THE NATURE OF EXPLANATION

THE
NATURE OF EXPLANATION

BY

K. J. W. CRAIK

M.A. (Edin.), Ph.D. (Camb.)

Fellow of St John's College, Cambridge

CAMBRIDGE

AT THE UNIVERSITY PRESS

1952

PUBLISHED BY
THE SYNDICS OF THE CAMBRIDGE UNIVERSITY PRESS

London Office: Bentley House, N.W.1
American Branch: New York

Agents for Canada, India, and Pakistan: Macmillan

First Edition 1943
Reprinted 1952

First printed in Great Britain at the University Press, Cambridge
Reprinted by offset-litho by Bradford & Dickens

CONTENTS

PREFACE

I am unhappy at the thought of presenting yet another philosophy. There have been so many statements of reality with a personal twist—outlines of philosophy, science, sociology or religion—and such varied interpretations of dead writers. No one ever seems quite satisfied with anyone else's views.

Again, an author relies largely on his feelings of the 'roundedness' and satisfactoriness of his own theory; he feels it strengthened by each new problem which occurs to him and appears to find an answer in terms of it, just as a good scientific theory finds confirmation in meeting new facts successfully. But in a theoretical study such as philosophy the new facts which present themselves are determined more by one's mental make-up than by an impartial sampling of reality; for it is association rather than experience which presents them. So even this 'coherence test of truth' may indicate, as perhaps it does in the case of Kant's 'architectonic', not so much the objective validity of the theory as the groove in which the author's mind runs. Instead of his theory being as wide as reality, his perception of reality may be as narrow as his theory.

Besides, if my view of the deceptiveness of verbal precision happens to be correct, the analysis of apparently definite perceptual situations or concepts stirs up a bottomless morass where statement becomes increasingly difficult and judgment more uncertain. Yet is it not possible that some definite contribution to the solution of philosophical problems may come from the application of the various experimental methods which have advanced the sciences? It may be that some—particularly ontological—problems are not open to such treatment; but it seems to me that the peculiar difficulty of philosophical problems is only increased by the employment of methods of description and explanation which would fail to give a satisfactory account of physical phenomena, a considerable understanding of whose mechanism *can* be communicated by one person to another by suitable means. This problem will be discussed in connection with 'false hypostatisation', the theory of implication as a system of 'artificial causation' and the 'paralleling' theory of thought.

I am grateful to Dr Alice Heim for reading the original and clarifying the English in many places.

KENNETH J. W. CRAIK

February 1943

THE NATURE OF EXPLANATION

INTRODUCTION

The present state of philosophy

PHILOSOPHY seems at present to be in a stage of transition between the *a priorism* of the past and perhaps an experimental philosophy in the future. Thus, much of the old *a priorism* has been shaken off; the advances of the positive sciences have shown that the data of Aristotelian, Platonic, or Berkeleian days were less adequate than those now available for considering the relation between nervous and mental processes, the nature of the atom and of causal conjunctions, the type of visual perception found in adults who have regained their sight by corneal grafting and so forth. No one would now dare to draw up a list of self-evident but not tautologous propositions nor to derive a philosophical system from them by deduction as Spinoza did, and some caution is shown even in the reification previously so common—the talk of the self and its simplicity. The positive sciences have introduced their own methodology—induction supported by experiments to test hypotheses. The fundamental feature of such procedure is that it is never necessary to be sure that the conditions have been defined with complete exactness and finality—indeed, it is recognised that this is impossible. Rather the aim is to do experiments, described as exactly as possible, and lay the emphasis on the fact that they work— that they fulfil predictions, or confirm other experiments. The importance of a theory lies not in the degree of finality attained by definition and analysis, but in the power and grasp of general principles appearing in diverse instances. Advances in the design of wireless sets lie not in the exactness with which a valve is defined but in the faithfulness with which the original sound is reproduced or the range of the set, and the same applies even in the most theoretical aspects of physics: the aim is extensive (though not in the sense of formal) rather than intensive—to cover a multitude of facts so that they appear familiar and predictable and to be able to say: 'I told you what would happen, and I was right; I will tell you again, and I shall probably be right.' This procedure has, of course, been made the basis of various types of philosophy—of pragmatism, positivism, and to some extent of operationalism; indeed, it has been overdone; sometimes the practical aspect has been so emphasised as to suggest that nothing really exists except the actual experimental procedures used by scientists, and that even they can prove the existence of nothing except their own experiments! But the likelihood remains that physics has proceeded successfully without a philosophy just because its experimental procedure is, in some way which we shall examine in more detail later, self-verifying and self-justifying, and philosophy had better ask whether the same does not apply to itself. Perhaps one function of philosophy is to consider the nature of this self-validation. The point where philosophy at the moment shows its old *a priorism* is in its search for rigid definitions and reification without contradiction. The philosophy of perception seeks description in terms of the observer and the object observed; and to avoid falling into difficulty with errors, hallucinations, sensory abnormalities, differences in previous experience and so forth, it is led to postulate further entities such as sense-data whose realm of existence is extremely uncertain. When driven into a corner it seeks refuge in still greater rigidity of definition. For instance, it may escape into the strict formalism of Russell and Whitehead's symbolic logic—a garden where all is neat and tidy but bearing little relation to the untidy tangle of experience from which the experimentalist tries to derive his principles. Or it may fly to the somewhat similar confines of logical positivism where, again, the difficulties are attributed to the inexact or ambiguous use of words, and it is implied that their use in one or more exactly defined senses will save the situation, and if this seems to restrict the range of problems somewhat—well, it cannot be helped. It is this effort at still greater rigidity of definition which is, in my view, the fundamental error, though I hope later to show why it should be so great a temptation. It seems to contradict the fundamental lesson learned from the positive sciences—namely, that you can never prove the existence of any external thing, or its obedience to a particular law, by trying to wring the truth out of a particular example; you must vary the conditions, repeat the experiments, make a hypothesis and a remote inference from that hypothesis and test it out. In any particular experiment some unforeseen factor may be at work; you cannot safely pick up a single stone, pass it to a friend and say: 'There, in your hand, you hold a perfect example of the law of gravitation; analyse its behaviour, and you will know all.' On the contrary, the earthward pull of that particular stone may be partly due to magnetic iron ore in it. If we let it fall, its rate of descent will not be simply due to its acceleration under gravity but will be reduced by air resistance. Its mass cannot be determined with perfect exactness and may vary with humidity, erosion of its surface and so on. It is only by taking numerous examples and tracking down the problem from all sides that we can extract the truth; we can never wring it out of the particular example. Even if, when our knowledge is considerable, we can specify a fairly 'perfect' example—e.g. a lump of gold falling in a vacuum—this is merely the result, not the means, of our knowledge, and our perfect example may prove only to be one of many imperfect, indirect approaches to the next unknown problem where again we cannot prescribe and define exactly. Surely the philosophical method of exact definition and unambiguous statement makes exactly this error. It tries to 'pin down' the problem to a single instance; it says, 'Here am I, myself, perceiving a stick', and proceeds to define perception as the observation of sense-data, which forces us to the conclusion that I may be really and truly perceiving the stick in the aforesaid sense, but that I know very little about the stick, compared with what the positive sciences have told me. The trouble, perhaps, is that the positive sciences are often alluded to as the *exact* sciences, and that they do, indeed, inherit a number of apparently precise definitions from their complacent past. But every day these definitions—for instance of force, mass and velocity in terms of each other for the purposes of mechanics—prove slightly inapplicable to 'real' force, mass and velocity as new facts such as relativity effects are found by experiment. The old definitions still serve a useful purpose—more useful, often, than their more modern and complicated counterparts. This perhaps is the root of the matter: scientists and philosophers alike are distressed that inexact definitions should work well, both for practical and theoretical purposes. Whenever a paradox *does* arise, they attribute it to this inexactness, which is partially correct; but they fail to see that their remedy of exact definition may be impossible and unattainable by the very nature of the physical world and of human perception, and that their definition should be corrected in the way of greater extensiveness and denotative power, rather than greater analytical, intensive or connotative exactitude. For instance, when the perception or the description of reality meets with difficulties such as the paradoxes of error and illusion the philosopher should not retire within his own fortress, withdraw his brave claims to be knowing reality, and defend bitterly a few strongholds such as the self and sense-data. Rather he should launch out and try to gain widespread support for his theory of perception by linking it with physiological and physical processes, and making vague but general alliances with the great world of facts outside him. Then, gradually, will come self-verification—the advance of a theory of which we can say, 'Yes, it works.' We shall be unable to say rigidly what we mean by 'yes', or 'it', or 'works', but the fact will remain that something is happening—a theory and a group of general principles are holding true and being fulfilled in a way which is almost infinitely improbable if there is no causality. There will always remain the opportunity for investigating the nature of principles, and the meaning of such ideas as that of principles 'working' or 'holding true', but the final road to progress will lie not in the search for analytical exactitude in verbal definition but in the self-validatory procedure of experiment and hypothesis. The important feature of a concept is that it should be exact *in the right way*—i.e. true—not just internally precise.

Finally, I do not think it is philosophy alone but science also which needs an experimental philosophy; for, although specific discoveries will continue to be made by particular sciences there are many experimental problems—such as the relation between nervous activity and thought, between physiological conditions and mental disease, between abnormal physical and physiological conditions and error or illusion—which are unlikely to be tackled by the pure psychologist or the pure physiologist, but are likely to be as fruitful as many other 'border-line sciences' like astrophysics or biochemistry. The general philosophical outlook coupled with a desire to establish results experimentally may bridge this gap between physiology and psychology.

CHAPTER I

The function and importance of explanation. Discussion of some current theories

WHAT do we mean by 'explaining' anything? This is a problem of considerable theoretical and practical importance. First of all, every science is concerned with explanation, and it should be as important to ask what is being *done*, in attempting to explain a phenomenon, as to ask what particular explanation is most satisfactory. Secondly, it has practical importance in that men differ as to what explanations are satisfactory, and whether it is necessary ever to go beyond the bounds of one science to find a satisfactory explanation of a phenomenon which at first sight seems clearly to belong to that science.

Perhaps the hardest blow was struck at the theory of explanation by Hume and later by quantum physicists. Previously, it had at least been held that explanation was concerned with finding the causes of events. Hume denied that we could ever point to any idea of 'causality', i.e. 'necessary connection' as apart from mere continual succession; and modern physics seems to say, in effect, that it has no use for causality since causality would hold only for immeasurable quantities and unobservable objects, if it held at all; and the purpose of science is taken to be the making of verifiable statements and predictions, rather than hypotheses about unobservables.

It is possible that the meaning of 'explanation' is different for different people; it may be one of those things which no one really understands, but which every scientist, or anyone else in a mood of curiosity, feels he desires. His particular ideal, felt rather than known, determines the kind of experiments he will choose to do, and the kind of answer he will accept. Nevertheless, there is a large field of explanation that is common to most men. Explanations are not purely subjective things; they win general approval, or have to be withdrawn in the face of evidence and criticism; and the man who can explain a phenomenon understands it, in the sense that he can predict it, and utilise it more than other men.

The question why one explanation or another should seem satisfactory involves the prior question why any explanation at all should be sought after and found satisfactory. It is clear that, in fact, the power to explain involves the power of insight and anticipation, and that this is very valuable as a kind of distance-receptor in time, which enables organisms to adapt themselves to situations which are about to arise. Apart from this utilitarian value it is likely that our thought processes are frustrated by the unique, the unexplained and the contradictory and that we have an impulse to resolve this state of frustration, whether or not there is any practical application. I shall give in Chapters V and VI a hypothetical explanation of this impulse, which may be experimentally verified or disproved in the course of time.

There are, then, five main attitudes to the problems of knowledge and explanation: *A priorism*, which asserts certain facts and principles to be self-evident or certain, and deduces a great body of supposed knowledge therefrom; *Scepticism*, which denies the legitimacy of these first principles, and questions some or all of the foundations of the belief in an external world and causal interaction; *Descriptive* theories, which assert that explanation is 'generalised description' but never tells us anything about the causes of events; *Relational* theories (represented by modern physics), which declare themselves to be uninterested in whether causal action between supposed ultimate units may be taking place, on the ground that things are unobservable and hence unpredictable; and that the aim of science is to find relations between observable entities which are constantly obeyed and hence permit successful predictions to be made. The foundation of this method is the association of definite probabilities, smaller than unity, with events. Finally, there are *Causal* theories, which hold that the events we see are the consequences of the interaction of external objects according to definite and certain rules.

Let us examine these different theories in turn, not with a view to establishing the validity of any one beyond all doubt, but to justify the pursuit of an experimental method.

CHAPTER II

A priorism *and scepticism*

DISTINCTIONS have often been drawn between philosophy and the positive sciences on the grounds both of subject-matter and method. It is certainly true that philosophy considers various ontological and epistemological problems with which, so far, the positive sciences have hardly concerned themselves; but philosophy has also been characterised since its earliest days by an *a priori* or rationalist approach. Such is the assertion of certain principles concerning reality as self-evident or the implicit assumption of them and the deduction of conclusions therefrom. There are certainly degrees of *a priorism*, and a modern tendency for caution in the enunciation of first principles. As remarked above, it is doubtful whether anyone would now dare to advance so complete a deductive system as Spinoza, and the ontological and cosmological arguments for the existence of God find little acceptance. Yet I think one can show that there is an astonishingly strong current of *a priorism* in the more modern types of philosophy—in empiricism, scepticism, subjectivism, phenomenalism, and logical positivism, and the theory of emergent evolution. The last, in Bergson's hands, postulates the existence of an *élan vital* for which there is no compelling evidence; but we shall consider this theory in more detail in connection with the possibilities of mechanical organisation in Chapter VI. The others, though more cautious in their claims, assert or assume the legitimacy of certain analyses of experience. Many philosophers, including Descartes, Hume, Berkeley and Whitehead, are characterised by their confident introspective analysis of experience. In the following section some quotations from their works are taken and discussed.

DESCARTES'S *DISCOURSE ON METHOD*
(Everyman Edition)

Descartes's criterion of objective reality—to be able to conceive a thing clearly and distinctly—is very ambiguous; it might mean the recognition of an idea as consistent with the greater part of our other knowledge, which is the coherence test of truth; or it might mean an almost emotional satisfaction with the results of introspection. In fact, it seems to have meant the two, confused together, since he was both a great physicist (as in his discovery of the cause of rainbows) and a very keen advocate of the self-evidence of certain propositions which are synthetic, i.e. stating something positive about the nature of independent reality.

P. 27. 'I supposed that all the objects that had ever entered into my mind when awake had in them no more truth than the illusions of my dreams. But immediately upon this I observed that, whilst I wished to think that all was false, it was absolutely necessary that I, who thus thought, should be somewhat; and as I observed that this truth, *I think, hence I am*, was so certain and of such evidence, that no ground of doubt, however extravagant, could be alleged by sceptics capable of shaking it, I concluded that I might, without scruple, accept it as the first principle of the philosophy of which I was in search.' But, as Lindsay remarks (p. xix): 'What is really implied in the fact of doubting is a subject that doubts. Descartes assumes without proof that a subject that doubts must have personal identity, or must be what he calls a substance.' Surely the fact is that Descartes applied *a priori* notions in a realm where we should be more cautious, with modern knowledge of dissociation and 'split-personality' and of the multitude of separate living cells that compose us, interdependent in varying degrees and some remarkably self-supporting, and that he was just incapable of thinking that the self might not be what it seemed to his introspections. He could see further than most men of his time—he reflected on his veridical and illusory perceptions; but he could not take the next step and see that even he who saw, and his act of seeing, might be an example of unity and simplicity in complexity, and that these concepts of the self, of existence, and of doubting were themselves as inexact and as suspicious as the concept of an object perceived in space. Most philosophers must have had the experience of thinking they had solved a problem while criticisms still waited to be sprung on them and unsuspected weaknesses in their armour detected by their opponents. That, surely, is what happened to Descartes; he showed a philosophic insight into the suspicious nature of single observations of the external world; he saw that naïve realism will not work; but he failed to see that the same applies to introspection—there he was a naïve realist still.

HUME, *A TREATISE OF HUMAN NATURE*
(Everyman Edition)

P. 94. 'Thus, not only our reason fails us in the discovery of the *ultimate connection* of causes and effects, but even after experience has informed us of their *constant conjunction*, it is impossible for us to satisfy ourselves by our reason, why we should extend that experience beyond those particular instances which have fallen under our observation.'

P. 95. 'We have no other notion of cause and effect but that of certain objects, which have been *always conjoined* together, and which in all past instances have been found inseparable. We cannot penetrate into the reason of the conjunction. We only observe the thing itself, and always find that, from the constant conjunction, the objects require a union in the imagination.'

Pp. 164–5. The idea of necessary connection is attributed to 'the propensity' of the mind 'to spread itself on external objects, and to conjoin with them any internal impressions which they occasion'.

His discussion of the rules by which we judge causes and effects, e.g. p. 170, is of course very clear and concise, just as is Berkeley's account of the visual cues for distance—a curious paradox that subjectivists should so clearly state some of the objective data which physiological and psychological processes utilise.

BERKELEY, *FIRST DIALOGUE OF HYLAS AND PHILONOUS*
(Everyman Edition, p. 233)

Hyl. Do we not perceive the stars and moon, for example, to be a great way off? Is not this, I say, manifest to the senses?

Phil. Do you not in a dream too perceive those or like objects?

Hyl. I do.

Phil. And have they not then the same appearance of distance?

Hyl. They have.

Phil. But you do not thence conclude the apparitions in a dream to be without the mind?

Hyl. By no means.

Phil. You ought not therefore to conclude that sensible objects are without the mind, from their appearance or manner wherein they are perceived.

Hyl. I acknowledge it.

Berkeley chooses his situation so as to avoid the issue of the truth or falsity of a perception and its relation to consistency. He ignores the fact that a person's dreams are not, in fact, internally consistent for long, and, even when this occurs, they are not consistent with any other person's except on the rarest occasions. In other words, the probability of the dream-systems of the whole world being consistent with each other day in and day out is vanishingly small, whereas this consistency goes on in our perceptions of the actual world. Admittedly one may think two items in a dream, or two illusory sensations, to be consistent when they are not—for instance if one is drunk or fatigued or insane; but other people will point out our error. Admittedly also in ourselves and in other people this judgment that two experiences are consistent with each other is a subtle thing, based partly on feeling and inarticulate thought, and is easily disturbed by any abnormal bodily condition; but in the majority of cases it tends to be right because, I shall argue, it is based on and moulded by the consistent processes of the outer world and all the inconsistencies and errors and illusions enter subsequently, in the mechanism of our mind; that at least is my hypothesis. This justifies continual trial and experiment and observation by numerous people as the only sure criterion. Any one man is more likely to be right if he makes many observations than if he makes one observation; but even if he makes many he may put a warped interpretation on them—for instance, he may think them all to be consistent with some esoteric theory of his own; and nothing but the evidence of other men will help to show him reality and to keep him in the way of sanity.

MAIN POINTS IN WHITEHEAD'S *PRINCIPLES OF NATURAL KNOWLEDGE*

Whitehead, also, seems to lay a false emphasis on definition and ideas of what it, and deductive reasoning, can accomplish. The fact that he talks of events rather than of other entities does not avoid the difficulty. Why should we take it on ourselves to define a material object as 'continuous in space and time' (p. 182) and then conclude that we are wrong in classifying a drop of water as a material object? 'Such paradoxes', he continues (p. 183), 'mean that vital distinctions have been overlooked. We must distinguish between the drop of water as it appears, the event which is its situation, and the character of the event which causes the event to present that appearance. Namely, there is the appearance of the drop of water.' It is true, I think, that the occurrence of a paradox generally means that we have failed to make a necessary distinction; but the remedy is generally an experimental investigation of the real event we are trying to describe rather than a logical distinction which only appears to separate the warring alternatives. He betrays the same longing for verbal precision in complaining (pp. 183–4) that 'the line of separation between delusive and non-delusive perceptual objects is not quite so clear as we might wish'. Whitehead notes the 'fallacy of misplaced concreteness'— e.g. the categories of substance and attribute—which is the same as the fallacy of hypostatisation; yet he himself commits this fallacy in his isolation and definition of single events.

MAIN POINTS FROM AYER'S *FOUNDATIONS OF EMPIRICAL KNOWLEDGE*

CHAPTER I. We must postulate sense-data rather than material objects because we may be subject to illusions in sense-perception. If, however, we always say that we are aware simply of the sense-datum no problem arises except as a result of ambiguous use of language ('ambiguous use of language' being thus his term for all attempts men have ever made, in art and science, to get outside themselves and know an objective, independent, physical reality). Sense-datum language is the most convenient, but not the only one—other theories of perception are 'alternative languages'.

CHAPTER 2. Mainly an attempt at precise formulation of sense-data in language.

CHAPTER 3. If we experience only sense-data we cannot know that other people exist (i.e. the surviving fragments of the idea that existence means verifiability and that the meaning of a proposition is the method of its verification still haunt him). The difficulty is evaded by including possible as well as actual experience. He refuses to admit that meaning, as a general term, can legitimately be discussed; only the meaning of particular propositions (cf. p. 98).

CHAPTER 4 is a rather indefinite kind of physics and mechanics of sense-data describing a few of their laws in a vague way. He is soon faced with anomalies which he does not attempt to resolve; he does not seem to realise that it is these very anomalies which have led physicists to seek some reality behind these sensations in case perchance they may show greater consistency, as in fact they do. His method is Phenomenalist. The existence of real occupants and physical objects is denied.

The most common of philosophical assumptions are:
(1) That the way of escape from the inconsistencies of sense-experience lies in taking some particular event in sense-experience and formulating it in the most precise, yet cautious, terms;
(2) That among these methods of formulation, exact

definition and the description of things and events in substantival terms hold a foremost place;

(3) That, whatever we may question, we are entitled to employ words to express our questioning;

(4) 'Esse est percipi', or, in more sophisticated terms, 'the meaning of a proposition is the means of its verification', or existence and observability are co-extensive.

The first is characteristic of practically every philosophy, formalist or empiricist. Locke, Berkeley, Hume, Kant and Ayer all alike give introspective analyses of particular instances of perception, such as the seeing of an apple, of the passage of a steamer down-stream, or of a stick half under water. Exact definition of the particular case seems the first remedy to which they are all driven as soon as an illusion or error causes them to question naïve realism. But it is not the remedy of the ordinary man, nor of the physicist. The ordinary man does not question the reality of the external world when he finds that the stick seen under water is really straight; he only says that he was mistaken if he concluded it to be bent, from his first observation; and the physical scientist concludes that a single observation is never reliable; he repeats his experiments and employs different methods, and is only satisfied if all give consistent results. Many philosophers accept the coherence theory of truth, but few seem to consider its application to the analysis of perceptual experience. As mentioned in the introduction, you cannot wring the truth out of a particular observation of a particular event; the positive sciences have realised this long enough, though they give little explanation of why it should be so, and little explicit justification of our belief in the external world. So the attempt to evade contradictions by the exact observation and formulation of a particular sensory experience is open to doubt. Philosophers themselves sometimes realise these difficulties of exact observation. They find it hard to separate substance and attribute, to say where one thing ends and another begins, to deal with identity through change and so forth, and they may occasionally feel that they are less experienced in the methods of exact observation than physicists. They therefore turn to exact definition as a remedy. The outcome is the logistic of Whitehead and Russell, or the logical positivism of Moore, Broad, Ayer, etc., or the operationalism of Bridgeman, Stevens and others. The common feature of these is that they attribute all error and most unsolved philosophical problems to the inexact definition and use of terms or to illegitimate extensions of, and inferences from, them. This surely involves an *a priori* assumption—that the nature of the real must accord with our exact definitions. The remedy may lie in seeking to state the real exactly, rather than in seeking 'internal' exactness in definition. At first this may take the form of a claim that definitions, subjectively laid down, have objective validity with regard to an external, independent world; but the difficulty of showing how they can have this validity led Kant and all phenomenalists after him to claim instead that the real was as narrow as their definitions. Subjective definitions, in other words, have objective validity only because the supposedly objective is merely what is described by those subjective definitions! Admittedly the phenomenalists give a somewhat more sophisticated statement of their position, and evade all questions as to *where* sense-data exist, what status they have, or how they are related to each other and to us; but in essentials the answer is as above: objective validity simply means subjective validity for them.

There is a good deal of evidence that the precise definitions of the symbolical logicians and the logical positivists do not, in fact, cover very much of the range even of sensory experience, and cover none of it exactly. As Haldane (1938) remarks, logistic 'will only work for material that has certain highly abstract properties, which are rather less frequently and much less completely exemplified in the real world than logicians would like us to believe'. Again, most mathematical—not to mention physical—discoveries have emerged into comparative definiteness from a condition of meaningful obscurity. Thus, as Love (1926) remarks of the Infinitesimal Calculus: 'There was no need for this confused conception [of infinitely small quantities neither zero nor finite] and it came to be understood that it can be dispensed with. The calculus was not developed by its first founders in accordance with logical principles from precisely defined notions, and it gained adherents rather through the impressiveness and variety of the results that could be obtained by using it than through the cogency of the arguments by which it was established. A similar statement might be made in regard to other theories included in mathematical analysis, such, for instance, as the theory of infinite series. Many, perhaps all, of the mathematical and physical theories which have survived have had a similar history—a history which may be divided roughly into two periods: a period of construction, in which results are obtained from partially formed notions, and a period of criticism, in which the fundamental notions become progressively more and more precise, and are shown to be adequate bases for the constructions previously built upon them.' Again, Edgeworth (1926) remarks: 'As in other mathematical sciences, so in probabilities, or even more so, the philosophical foundations are less clear than the calculations based thereon.' Pledge (1939) also notes (in regard to the fifteenth century) that 'in all this much future knowledge was implicit. . . . These notions were not formulated until long after our period opens.' In physics, the exact definitions of mass, velocity and force (in terms of each other) to be found in text-books of mechanics have been gradually found to be slightly inapplicable to 'real' mass and velocity, though none the less useful for many practical purposes. In symbolic logic, the essential problem of logic—implication and inference—has been avoided by Moore's definition of material implication which has been condemned by Hawkins (1937) as 'an act of philosophical piracy', while 'entailment' is left to take its place and given little consideration. Presumably this is because entailment, or implication in the ordinary sense, involves the philosophically disreputable notion of empirical causal conjunction. Blanchard (1939), vol. II, p. 381, also notes 'the disparity between the highly artificial implication we have been describing and the implication of ordinary thought'. Foley (1937) has remarked on 'the fallacy of hypostatisation' by which objects and events are given a precision in words which they do not in fact possess. It is easy to quote examples showing that the methods of analytical philosophy would fail to describe and explain many phenomena which physical science can deal with effectively; that the philosophical method is no more satisfactory in its own territory; and that any apparent successes it may have are due rather to a 'psychological' than to an objective validity—an ability to forestall the obvious criticisms rather than to meet new data.

THE UNSUITABILITY OF SUBSTANTIVAL LANGUAGE

We must consider whether the language of philosophy and psychology is not unsuitable for expressing their problems. It uses nouns freely to designate immutable substances, incapable of coming out of nowhere or of changing into one another or ceasing to exist; and these substances are in consequence sharply delimited from one another. An attempt is made to prove the self and other substances to be simple lest complexity should suggest any continuity between their

categories. When we examine physical reality, as now understood, we find that very few of the 'things' which we
denominate by nouns show these properties. Energy or
matter or both together are conserved, and do not appear
to come from nowhere or pass into nothingness; but all
their combinations into higher units or 'things' *are* capable
of changing into one another, and, in a sense, of coming
out of nothing; for they can arise from a mass of units so
dissimilar as to seem incapable of producing them. A mass
of iron ore is so unlike an engine that the uninitiated might
disbelieve that an engine could ever be made from it. In
the same way, consciousness seems so unlike matter that
many deny that it can possibly arise from it; they say that
unless one admits consciousness as a fundamental substance
one is 'denying' it altogether.

Darwin makes the same point in his *Origin of Species*, empha-
sising that most men are unwilling to admit the possible unity
of two different things unless they see the transitional stages.

THE EFFECT OF FALSE HYPOSTATISATION
IN EXPLANATION

This hypostatisation leads to a number of difficulties which
are not peculiar to philosophy and psychology, but which
psychologists and philosophers often think are so. If we
tried to describe the working of a motor engine in terms of
the intake, the change of intake to compression, the tendency
of the gas, in a Diesel, to explode as it is more and more
compressed, the moment of explosion, and so on, we should
find ourselves faced with many of the difficulties of philosophy—what the explosion was before the moment of
combustion, how it has come to exist out of nowhere, where
it exists and what is its status, what is the status of a 'tendency'
to explode, in what sense the engine is more than a collection

of atoms of metal and other material, in what sense it is simple or complex, and so forth. These are almost the same as the problems of the self and its status, of the nature and mode of existence of sense-data or concepts, the nature of organisation or of tendencies and potentialities. Maybe there is more organisation, and a new kind of simplicity and unity in the living organism; but this possibility seems to me no reason for handicapping ourselves by trying to explain living processes in language that could not describe non-living ones. We might at least take the difficulties singly. It is as if we started to describe a race by a geometrical series of diminishing steps, as in the paradox of Achilles and the tortoise, saying that Achilles ran a yard, then half a yard, then a quarter, and so on. It would take an infinite time to describe the race up to the point at which Achilles passed the tortoise. This would not mean that there was any real paradox or inconsistency; for in fact he has, in the same sense, an infinite time—a succession of geometrically diminishing time intervals—in which to accomplish this. But our time-perception, and our description of events, consists of a series of arithmetically equal steps, and such a series is more suited to the description of what we see, and provides an easier method of deciding by theory what events can occur and what can not. In the same way, I am not saying that the philosophical problems are unreal or are founded upon absolute misstatement; they must have some answer. But it seems important not to believe them peculiar to psychology or metaphysics, and important first to find some convenient method of describing the parts of mechanical processes which are understood, and see how far it assists in the explanation of psychological problems. Then one can go on to discuss how the other, paradox-producing, methods of statement have arisen, and why the problems so framed are difficult to answer clearly.

It may be objected that such a theory of the 'fuzziness' of reality (or 'mix-up-edness' as it has been called) and the slight inapplicability and inadequacy of all concepts conflicts with the principle of non-contradiction. But I agree that *if* an object is *A* it cannot at the same time be not-*A*; I only insist on the difficulty of deciding that an object *is A*, where *A* is a concept having any meaning through its relation to other concepts. Thus to call an animal *X* conveys nothing, and it is true to say, then, that it is not not-*X*, for the purpose in hand; but to call it a dog is a very much more serious undertaking, since this word has meaning already, and our animal may prove to be an embryo dog, or some hitherto unknown hybrid sharing the biological definitory characteristics both of dogs and not-dogs.

It may be replied, of course, that to seek a kind of language capable of describing processes which are generally agreed to be understood, is skating over the difficulties—that it will not reveal actual problems and paradoxes, and that we should employ the language which raises the most problems and difficulties. Surely a middle course must be steered; we do not want to avoid difficulties, but we do not want language to introduce incompatibility or variability where the physical events it is describing run smoothly and regularly. In general, the language of causality seems the most fruitful and successful and the language of substance, or existence and immutability, the least.

THE PROBLEMS OF PHILOSOPHY

Philosophy has proved better at propounding problems than at answering them; it has exhibited the difficulties of causality and of space and time, the problems of the existence of colours, secondary properties, and images, of free-will and moral qualities, of the relation between body and mind and of the nature of objects, relations and universals.

Two main methods of treatment have been applied to all these. One is sceptical, and consists simply in revealing the ambiguities and contradictions of our ordinary thinking on these matters. It is useful in showing where problems lie, and in revealing the inadequacy of our ordinary treatment, but it cannot provide the positive satisfaction of physical science which exhibits relations and recurrences and gives power to predict future events.

The positive answers advanced to these problems have not been very satisfactory. They have generally been attempts to resolve the inconsistencies by showing that some everyday propositions about objects are false or ambiguous or meaningless. The result seems to allay the criticism of the author and his readers to some extent, but the method rarely suggests any test of validity, such as is demanded of hypotheses in physics.

There is certainly a temptation to isolate objects, processes, colours, sense-data, images and so forth just because they *seem* to be fairly definite resting points for our mental processes and our perception of the physical world. But this fact that our minds, in dealing with processes that are 'fuzzy' in time and space, manage to isolate and hypostatise them just sufficiently to see their relevance to the bringing about of other processes, similarly treated, does not mean that this method of isolation and hypostatisation can be carried on indefinitely. The fact that the concepts of steam and water can be grasped sufficiently firmly by someone's mind to enable him to devise a condensing steam engine does not mean that either of those concepts will bear infinitely close examination. This is different from the position of mathematicians and symbolic logicians who hold, in general, that any successful reasoning entails the absolute precision of some concepts and relations, however abstract; and they find artificial examples which illustrate their point. The distinction is made by Pascal who remarks (*Pensées*, no. 1) that in mathematical thought 'the principles are palpable, but removed from ordinary use; so that for want of habit it is difficult to turn one's mind in that direction; but if one turns it thither ever so little, one sees the principles fully, and one must have a quite inaccurate mind who reasons wrongly from principles so plain that it is almost impossible they should escape notice.

'But in the intuitive mind the principles are found in common use and are before the eyes of everybody. One has only to look, and no effort is necessary; it is only a question of good eyesight, but it must be good, for the principles are so subtle and so numerous that it is almost impossible but that some escape notice.' It is arguable, however, that what he calls 'intuitive thought' or 'good eyesight' plays a much larger part in knowledge of external reality than he might admit.

I shall try in Chapters V and VI to give a hypothetical explanation of how it comes about that we should be so tempted to analyse and hypostatise nature in this way, and why it is, in fact, very important for us to do so, up to a point, both in ordinary and scientific thinking.

In Chapter VII some types of experimental verification are suggested. The ontological problems still remain. Some of them (i.e. whether mind as a completely new 'entrant' need be postulated) would find some answer, perhaps, in terms of our model; so might some of the problems of the apprehension of relations, etc., and of the origin of verbal paradoxes, meaningless questions, etc. But the truly ontological questions still remain. Some problems must always be unanswerable; it is probably impossible to expound the nature of space or time to any great extent. Physics has, however, gone a long way in showing what are 'ultimates' and elements, what things are most permanent and what spatial relations are possible.

CONSEQUENCES OF *A PRIORISM*

The ordinary man asserts that he sees an external world containing various objects. It is only the philosopher who insists that he is conscious of sense-data, brown patches, and so forth. It is, curiously enough, *a priorism*—the endeavour to obtain the greatest certainty—which leads to the greatest ignorance of the real nature of things, and, carefully followed out, even to admission of ignorance, in scepticism. For the philosopher who is willing to stake everything on assertions such as 'I experience colours and other sensations and nothing else' can never prove that these sensations are attributable to external objects or that there is any causal connection between these events. If this analysis into sense-data were inevitable, we should certainly be unable to prove externality and causal connection; but this analysis into sensa has, in fact, never been proposed except as a means of philosophical escape from the problems of perception—and physiology and physics between them provide an alternative, and much richer method of investigating many essential stages in the perceptual process.

A priorism leads either to mere dogmatic assertion of some propositions about sense-data or experience, or, logically followed out, to utter scepticism, just because it starts from a false and inadequate statement of reality and experience. Thus the phenomenalist, the Cartesian, and the subjectivist question the certainty of each particular experience in turn and seek some particular experience which shall be certain. They give no reason for thus seeking certainty in the particular instance rather than in general laws. They finally decide that some proposition, such as that I am experiencing a red sense-datum, or that I exist, is certain. Surely they fail to realise that it is only a very few parts of experience that can be stated even with this degree of apparent certainty. For instance, most objects are so indefinite in colour and their colour so dependent on shadows and reflections that it is exceedingly difficult to give a definite description of the supposed sense-data. But, further, I do not see how they can cope, even in their chosen instances, with several difficulties. What happens, for instance, if I make a verbal error and say that there is a green sense-datum when I mean a red one? What proves me wrong except consistency with other people's experience or my own at different times? Further, how does the phenomenalist—Mr Ayer for instance—justify his use of words at all? How, for instance, does he know that, at any particular moment, he has not started talking gibberish instead of English? How does he know that the printer will, in general, print the same words that he has written? Or how does he know that words have any power at all to represent experiences, or to represent and recall the same experiences at the next moment? It seems to me that the possibility of verbal error must lead the phenomenalist to recoil even from statement of his own sense-data to the more general statement that he is seeing what he is seeing at any moment. Then again, his inability to justify the assumption that words can represent things, or that words or sense-data retain any identity from moment to moment, must prevent him from assuming that words can represent sense-data at all, or that his hearers have in any way the same thoughts as he himself had when they read his writings. He must therefore be reduced not merely to the verbal statement of a sceptical outlook, but to a scepticism with regard to the power of words to express thought at all, or the power of thought to do anything, or be anything; he dare not even think; in other words....

Well, that silence is surely what he is reduced to. His original hope of finding something certain in some particular experience has led to paralysis of all thought and language and action, and to utter emptiness. As Northrop (1931) says: 'The consequence of Hume's analysis is neither probable nor pragmatic science, but no science.'

Having reduced the sceptic to silence can we not now begin to say something? We can make a noise when a certain event occurs and find that this naming of events does work[1] on the whole. Now and again we may be misled, but this does not drive ordinary men or physicists to disbelieve altogether in the possibility of knowledge of the external world. As a result of making noises in conjunction with things we build up language, and in using language we make the discovery that this symbolical representation of events does in fact work just as when somebody tells us that there is a train to London at a certain time we do usually find that the rest of our experiences conform with this prediction. This language is based on the assumption of external objects behaving in a certain way. The primary fact is that we have discovered something by observation and experiment—we have discovered that symbols can work and can predict our future experience. Even our use of words to express this discovery is based on the same discovery. If symbolism did not work we could never express the fact that it failed to work; but as it does work we can express the fundamental fact that it does, and can say a great deal more besides. Thus we can surely silence the complete sceptic or the phenomenalist by pointing out that as soon as he opens his mouth to argue he is assuming that words can symbolise events, and that he is no better able to justify this assumption than the assumption he rejects—that words are able to represent external objects and events. Thus the use of language itself is based on the principle that any symbolism which works has objective validity; and it is illegitimate to use words to contradict this principle. Such

[1] See Chapter V for discussion of this concept.

usage merely indicates that the associative processes of thought are so devious and often so little conscious that some of their earlier steps are forgotten.

Probably most philosophers will object that the notion that symbolism 'works' is as obscure and dissatisfying as any *a priori* principle ever advanced. It is not in fact emotionally very satisfying. But, at the same time, it seems to me the one bridge between thought and the outer world; for it consists, formally, in saying: '*If* an outer world exists, then such and such a prediction of mine should come true; it does, therefore an outer world exists.' It means that it was *designed as a test for the existence of the outside world, and that it was fulfilled.* This criterion of fulfilment enables us to distinguish between legitimate and illegitimate hypotheses. If I say, 'If objects are all ideas specially created by God in my mind—God being free to put whatever ideas He wishes before my mind at any moment...' then I cannot make any hypothetical conclusion which can be proved true or false, and I therefore fail to bridge the gap between thought and external reality. But what are we to say of this process of implication—'*If* there is a stone, and *if* objects persist in the absence of external stimulation, *then* it should be there to-morrow'? What is the nature of this inference, and how are we to rule out hypotheses such as, 'If I am made of glass, the sun will rise to-morrow; the sun does rise to-morrow, therefore I am indeed made of glass'?

It is here that Mill's canons of induction assist us. To ensure that our hypothesis is correct it must say, '*If and only if* I am made of glass the sun will rise to-morrow', and this is not found to be experimentally true in that the sun will rise equally well on many other hypotheses. So the methods of agreement, difference and concomitant variation must all be used. The kind of hypotheses and of implication most employed may be roughly classified as those of Existence (e.g. if *A* exists, then we shall observe it again, if nothing interferes), of Position in time and space (e.g. if *A* is at present in this room I shall find it or him by examining the whole of the room), and of Cause and Effect (e.g. if *A* was produced by *B*, it should have such and such features, or if *A* produces *C* we should experience such and such events in the future).

Thus we do not try to *prove* the existence of the external world—we *discover* it, because the fundamental power of words or other symbols to represent events—the same power which is assumed by the sceptic who argues in favour of scepticism—permits us to put forward hypotheses and test their truth by reference to experience. This power of symbols to represent objects and events is thus the fundamental problem. It, too, is an experimental fact, and a fact which makes life possible. A particular type of symbolism may always fail in a particular case, as Euclidean geometry apparently fails to represent stellar space; but if all types of symbolism always failed, we should be unable to recognise any objects or exist at all.

CHAPTER III

Relational and descriptive theories

I KNOW that most quantum physicists would not accept the conclusions of this chapter. My own view is that I am not belittling any of their achievements or criticising any of the scientific consequences of the theory, but only their unwarranted extension from the field of observational methods and observational limitations to that of real existence and the limits of possibility. But if they remained unconvinced I hope they would not conclude that the succeeding chapters on possible mechanisms of thought were necessarily false, since these are advanced as mechanical hypotheses in regard to macroscopic events where statistical and causal theorists are agreed that mechanical laws hold very closely. There is only a difference in attitude to microscopic events where most quantum physicists regard indeterminism as a characteristic of real phenomena and I (tentatively, because I am unable to follow the mathematical detail of their theories) do not.

These theories, fashionable among modern physicists, admit that we can observe and predict regularities and conjunctions among events, but reject a causal interpretation, partly on the ground of Hume's scepticism, partly because the assumption of causality seems to be unnecessary when the association of probabilities with events appears to meet the case, and partly because Heisenberg's Uncertainty principle, interpreted as a principle of Indeterminacy in nature, seems to exclude rigid causality.

We have already suggested that the argument from scepticism is illegitimate on two grounds. First, it rests only on one particular method of stating experience which, as we shall see in discussing causality in Chapter IV, is not the only one. Secondly, it either assumes the validity of verbal and other forms of symbolism, in which case the symbolisation and discussion of external events is also legitimate, or it denies the possibility of symbolism at all, in which case it is reduced to silence and cannot express any meaning in any way. We have still to consider the arguments from the association of particular probabilities with events and from the Uncertainty principle.

The relational theory, in its modern physical form, associates definite probabilities with events on the basis of experiment and theory, and asserts that it is futile, meaningless, or illegitimate to go behind these probabilities to an underlying rigid causality. Thus, Born (1937) says: 'In the first place it is clear that the dualism, wave corpuscle, and the indeterminateness essentially involved therein, compel us to abandon any attempt to set up a *deterministic theory*. The *law of causation*, according to which the course of events in an isolated system is completely determined by the state of the system at time $t=0$, loses its validity, at any rate in the sense of classical physics. In reply to the question whether a law of causation still holds good in the new theory, two standpoints are possible. Either we may look upon processes from the pictorial side—in this case the law of causation certainly ceases to hold; or as is done in the further development of the theory, we describe the instantaneous state of the system by a (complex) quantity ψ which satisfies a differential equation, and which therefore changes with the time in a way which is completely determined by its form at time $t=0$, so that its behaviour is rigidly causal. Since, however, physical significance is confined to the quantity $|\psi|^2$ and others...which only partially define ψ, it follows that, even when the physically determinable quantities are completely known at time $t=0$, the initial value of the ψ-function is necessarily not completely definable. This view of the matter is equivalent to the assertion that events happen indeed in a strictly causal way, but that we do not know the initial state exactly. In this sense the law of causation is therefore empty; physics is in the nature of the case indeterminate, and therefore the affair of statistics.'

There are two important points here. First, Born does not justify his substitution of *indeterminism* for *uncertainty*. The physicists seem to have a curious belief that they have constructed things rather than discovered them. Neither the limit of observation imposed by the disturbing influence of the observing electron or quantum, nor the intangible nature of the conception of a wave-particle justifies us, surely, in imposing on reality the burden of supporting the shortcomings of our own intellects and instruments. Miss Stebbing (1937) makes the same criticism of Jeans and Eddington. It would have been very futile to deny the possible reality of electrical concomitants of nerve impulses a hundred years ago, just because there were no instruments capable of measuring them, and even though in the case of quanta we seem able to define the limit of observation with some accuracy, and to have no possible way of overcoming it, there seems no reason whatsoever for asserting that this range of uncertainty represents an indeterminateness in the interaction of the particles themselves.

Secondly, Born and the other statistical physicists consider themselves perfectly justified in associating definite probabilities with events while denying any causal basis for their occurrence. Is this legitimate? First, as has been argued by Montgomery, if we accept the validity of the theory of probability itself, but make no assumptions about causal interaction, any event is as likely to happen as any other, and the probability of the regular conjunctions which we experience day by day is almost infinitely small. One might add that the chance even of bodies persisting from day to day is small, and the chances of the laws of probability being obeyed *within* the system (as they are in fact) are still smaller if the whole system is a continuous instance of the occurrence of possible but almost infinitely improbable events. As Northrop (p. 284) remarks: 'Probability is meaningless apart from a given specific set of conditions, and if these conditions do not hold for more than a moment there is no means of determining the probability of a theory formulated in one decade and tested in the next. Unless the conditions which define probability hold independent of time, in short, unless there is some necessary relatedness that can be counted upon, even scientific theories are impossible.'

Secondly, apart from the legitimacy of associating particular probabilities with events in the absence of the assumption of causation, it seems to me that the whole theory of probability is ultimately founded on causal ideas—e.g. that white and red balls placed in a bag and shaken up shall continue to exist, shall remain red and white, and shall collide with one another according to rigid mechanical rules. If, instead of theorems about the sampling of balls in a bag the theory of probability were founded on the sampling of electrons in an interference fringe, with a view to saying which came through one slit and which through the other, we should be unable to perform the task of distinguishing them and unable therefore to derive any theory of probability at all. Thus I feel that the theory of probability is founded on these causal ideas and that it is meaningless to lop off the causality and hope to retain the notion of finite probabilities and to associate them with events. In the absence of the assumption of causality the whole notion of probability seems meaningless, and consequently it is also meaningless to say that one event is more probable than another. I have not been trying to prove by this means that causation exists, but only to show that any attempt to dispense with it is meaningless. The only way to prove that a thing exists, in my view, is to try out the hypothesis of its existence, in the way that will be considered in Chapters V and VI; the only reason for the foregoing arguments is to clear out of the way certain logical and philosophical objections which, in my view, are plausible only because the associative processes and assumptions involved in any train of thought are so involved that we are apt to try to lift ourselves up by our own boot-strings, and even to be convinced that we have succeeded, without ever realising what we are doing.

PROBABILITY

Laplace's principle that 'the probability of an event is the ratio of the number of cases which favour it to the number of all the possible cases, when nothing leads us to believe that one of these cases ought to occur rather than the others; which renders them, for us, equally possible', is a curious combination of psychological and mathematical and empirical conditions. This is no criticism of it. Rather, it shows that any such concept is an expression of the intricate relation between our brains, our thinking, and the external world, and could not have arisen *in vacuo*. I only want to show that it is so bound up with the external world and that the mathematician and the physicist have no right to cut themselves off from this world and continue to predict results from the theory of probability as if it were something separate.

The mathematician or physicist, if he continues to disclaim this dependence on causation, must claim either that the theory of probability is entirely *a priori* and yet has objective validity, or is empirical. In the first case, we meet with the usual difficulty: it is possible to devise a multitude of theories with a minimum of empirical basis, but there is no reason for preferring one to another. It would be possible to assert that the probability of m occurring among a number of events n is m^2/n or n/m instead of m/n, as on Laplace's theory. Only experience decides that his principle should be developed rather than any other, and in developing it by preference the mathematicians and physicists have shown their willingness to be influenced by the empirical. Secondly, it is possible to say that the basis of the theory of probability is entirely empirical—that it is simply a refinement of a convenient method of expressing the way in which events actually occur. It certainly is this. Our problem is whether this is all one can say, and whether it is legitimate to assert this without asserting something more about the relation between events. In the first place, there is often a confusion as to what is probable; conjunctions of events are probable; events are not. It is legitimate to say that the probability of an explosion following the application of a certain blow to a detonator is 0·9. It is meaningless to assert that the probability of the explosion occurring, in isolation, is 0·9. This already implies the influence of one event on another, for if events do not affect each other the probability of conjunctions[1] should be the product of the probabilities of the events themselves, and therefore smaller than the probability of either event alone occurring; whereas in fact the reverse is the case; if we find the conjunctions occurring often or always we find the component events occurring in isolation rarely or never. Again I am not drawing a sharp distinction between events and conjunctions of events; it is largely a matter of definition. But I do assert that *if* one defines an event so as to imply that it is isolated, uninfluenced and uninfluential, then probability is found to be inapplicable in

[1] E.g. of a quantum of light of an appropriate frequency striking a caesium plate *and* of a photoelectron emerging.

that case; whereas if we mean by an event a string of occurrences we find probability to be applicable to the relationship of the parts of that string; or if we talk of conjunctions of supposedly separable events, then again it is the relations of the events and their dependence on each other to which the theory of probability applies. Thus one cannot exclude the notion of ·influence and interdependence and continue to apply the notion of probability.

The same argument can be put in a different way. If we apply probability to events in isolation we are bound to admit that any event is as probable in succession to another as any other, and that the regular occurrences of events which we experience are almost infinitely improbable, though remotely possible. Now the theory of probability asserts that the occurrence of highly improbable events is an indication that the number of cases taken is too small to be significant, and that we cannot apply the theory of probability to them. Thus, again, if we try to apply the theory without assuming the interdependence of events we find that we are not entitled to use the theory, owing to the high improbability of our data. The conjunctions are probable only if one event definitely restricts the possible events that can happen after it—that is, if it influences subsequent events.

But we have not yet shown that there is rigid causation. It might be that ultimate events only exert an indeterminate influence on the next event so that it sometimes happens and sometimes does not, for no physical reason at all. To me this notion is almost meaningless. It is equivalent to saying that the same event, under the same conditions, does and does not affect another event. For on the theory of probability one instance does not affect the next; each is exactly like the last. The fact that a penny has fallen ten times head up does not in the least affect the next throw. So we are bound to admit that there is no reason why the first event should influence the next on some occasions and not on others. This is a lawlessness of which there has never been any positive evidence or analogy in experience, and I think any physicist, meeting such an occurrence on the macroscopic scale, would seek some difference in the conditions to account for the different result.

In the second place, probabilities imply higher probabilities behind them. Thus if, on the average, the shots on a target fall within a 6-inch circle the accuracy due to the charge alone without the unsteadiness of the marksman's arm would be higher, or the accuracy due to the marksman alone, without variations in the charge or in the wind, would be higher. Occasionally two factors may cancel out, but this will happen rarely when there are so many factors as to give a probability-scatter to the accuracy. On the average there will be a progressive reduction in the accuracy or the probability of exact conjunction between firing and a high degree of accuracy, the further we go from the ultimate (e.g. electronic) conjunctions.[1] (This is almost a restatement of the second law of thermodynamics.) It implies that the further we go back in tracing conjunctions the higher the probability of our finding regular conjunctions. Even if something sets a limit to observation we are entitled to assert that the next conjunction behind it, if we could observe it, would have a still higher probability than the one we observed.

None of these arguments is supposed to be a conclusive demonstration of the existence of causality. I do not believe any neat, verbal proof that would gain immediate assent can be found, for I think that the number of ideas behind apparently simple and isolable concepts such as that of probability is almost infinite. If this unknown background of

[1] I.e. since the probability of the total event is the product of the probabilities (all less than 1) of the component events.

thought and experience and physiological make-up produces concepts and at the same time conceals their origin it is highly unlikely that a few words will clear the confusion and indicate the true nature of the concept. All I have hoped to do, in support of my position, is to show various features of the concept of probability and its application which suggest that the notion of causal interaction lurks somewhere behind it all, and that to dispense with it is to resemble a prehistoric monster that starts to eat its own tail because its body is so unwieldy and its nervous system so slow and confused that it does not realise what it is doing.

I am not trying to belittle the achievements of quantum mechanics in covering and predicting phenomena. Clearly no other theory accounts satisfactorily for non-radiating states of electrons, for electron diffraction, black-body radiation distribution, etc. These effects suggested to Planck a definite hypothesis as to the nature of radiation which might well have been a modification of classical theories. Surely it is unfair to say, once and for all, that classical theories have failed because their assumptions as to the nature of radiation and the electron need modification. Either there is no discontinuity between classical and new theories, or there is a complete break such as the discovery of indeterminism in nature. The quantum physicists, on the whole, suggest the latter. Is this legitimate? There is no doubt at all that their hypotheses on the nature of radiation fit the facts better than any other; and there is also no doubt that they have encountered a seemingly insuperable obstacle to the exact observation of the mechanism of quantisation, emission, interference and so forth. There is also no doubt that in the face of this difficulty the statistical theory provides the best method of correlating observations and predicting new phenomena within a certain field. But every scientific hypothesis previous to this one has had two sides to its predictive power—it suggests both consequences, which the statistical quantum theory does, and causes or prior mechanisms, which the statistical quantum theory does not, since it explicitly limits itself in the last extreme by associating definite probabilities less than unity with events and rejecting the assumption of more ultimate processes with a probability of unity. If scientists had been content in macroscopic events to stop at this stage they would have failed to discover many things they have actually found. They would have rested content with saying that a type of tree had a 0.5 probability of surviving in a certain environment instead of trying to find, for instance, some salt which is so rare and unevenly distributed in that vicinity that only half the trees receive the required quantity of it. It is surely the search for a causal difference behind every difference in phenomena which has prompted every discovery. 'A is sometimes followed by B and sometimes not' is surely the final anomaly which, in every other branch of science, prompts further enquiry and gives in itself a sense of dissatisfaction rather than satisfaction; yet it is just at this point that quantum statistics stops. Of course the physicist will reply that the two cases are quite different; in that of the tree it is possible to advance a verifiable hypothesis as to the cause of the low rate of survival; in the case of atomic events it is not, owing to the Principle of Uncertainty. This lack of verifiability is an unfortunate fact but still does not justify, in my opinion, the confusion between a limit of observation and a limitation of existence. I am not asking physicists to make unverifiable hypotheses as to the nature of the electron (though some of these might suggest future experiments on a macroscopic scale); I am only asking them to refrain from saying that reality must have the same limitations as their methods of observation. Science surely is an attempt to find out the nature of reality by experiment, theoretical formulation of hypotheses, and verification; not an attempt to assert that reality has the same limitations as our methods of observation. This last is a kind of subjectivism into which science has fallen though it started out to be most objectivist, refusing to accept anything that was not verifiable. It is verifiability which is the fatal link. If a phenomenon is verifiable, it exists; but this does not mean that if it is not verifiable it does not exist. This is the old fallacy: 'All S are P, therefore all P are S.' The verifiability of statistical predictions shows that the statistical laws are true—that actual objects do behave according to these laws; but it certainly does not prove that these are the ultimate laws which they obey and that there may not be more ultimate mechanisms. Science is not reality; it is a method of investigating reality. So it is surely reasonable to ask the quantum physicist to refrain from asserting that unverifiable = meaningless and non-existent.

CHAPTER IV

On causality

IN the last chapter we proposed some arguments against purely relational or sceptical views of knowledge which were at the same time arguments in favour of the existence of causal interaction among external events. We may now discuss other statements of reality.

First, although Hume asserts that our experience contains only 'impressions and ideas' and states (p. 94) that 'we only observe the thing itself, and always find that, from the constant conjunction, the objects require a union in the imagination', it is equally legitimate to assert with White-head, for instance (p. 11), 'The essential point of his [Kant's] method is the assumption that "significance" is an essential element in concrete experience. The Berkeleyan dilemma starts with tacitly ignoring this aspect of experience, and thus with putting forward, as expressing experience, conceptions of it which have no relevance to fact,' and again (p. 12), '"Significance" is the relatedness of things. To say that significance is experience, is to affirm that perceptual knowledge is nothing else than an apprehension of things in their relations and as related.' A similar interpretation is given by Kemp-Smith. Both assert that Hume's statement of the *given* is at fault. These are good pleas for a fair and impartial facing of facts; but they fall short in that they rest ultimately on a kind of introspective analysis of experience whose adequacy must depend largely on the width of experience, impartiality, and honesty of the individual. Hume would just deny the existence of this relatedness in his experience, as some deny and others affirm their direct experience of God. Introspection is not enough. We must have some kind of experimental test which says: 'If we assume this to be the case, what will follow, and how can we test it?' As remarked before, one cannot expect a formal demonstration or deductive argument showing the existence of causal interaction; it must be established by the hypothetical and experimental method, by saying 'If causality held, this would happen, and would not happen if it did not hold; it does happen, so causality does hold'. Argument can only be expected to clear away rival arguments. There is one additional argument which seems to me·to indicate the interaction of objects in a few instances. I do not mean that it is a way of demonstrating the existence of causality, but only that it shows some of our words and concepts to be so pervaded and saturated with causality that no formal analysis, however rigorous, will rid them of causality and fit them to Humean atomism. Hume would deny that relatedness is given, or given in any such sense as to imply or establish necessary connection. But there is one relation which is characteristic of the given and appears more promising, namely, spatial relation. Our commonest 'experience' of causality is in the case where objects obstruct or support one another or in some other way influence each other because of their inability to pass through each other or occupy the same place at the same time. But the matter is not quite so simple as this. Two gases or solids may occupy the same space as one previously did (at the same pressure, in the case of the gases) after chemical combination. Electric and magnetic fields may occupy the same space apparently independently. The space occupied by an electron appears to be indefinite and to vary according to whether one is considering the space in which its electrical field or its mass make themselves felt. The atomic nucleus is apparently no larger than one proton or electron, though it may eject many. The notion of occupying space therefore requires modification; but it does seem true to say that two objects (or let us call them 'alterations' to cover the case of electric and magnetic fields, electro-magnetic waves, wave-packets, etc.) *of the same kind* never occupy the same space at the same time. Two of the most fundamental principles of modern physics, the Pauli exclusion principle and the principle of Interference, seem, so far as I can judge, to reinforce this statement. No energy is dissipated where two wave-trains 180° out of phase and of equal amplitude coincide—each appears to act as a perfect reflector to the other, for the amplitude in the in-phase fringes is twice, and the energy therefore four times, that of one beam alone. Thus, it would seem that while different types of 'alterations' of a given point in space are possible at the same time—e.g. electric, magnetic and gravitational fields—two of the same kind cannot coexist at the same place and time. If this be the case, there is thus something in the modern concept of an 'object' which includes the affecting of other objects; it places restrictions upon the possible places where they can exist, and thus shows itself in many macroscopic instances as simple solidity. This seems to be similar to the principle of non-contradiction that a thing cannot both be and not be something at the same time. Surely there is in the concept of an object this very power of affecting other objects, or causal property.

Macroscopic causation seems to rest on two main principles—the inability of two similar bodies to occupy the same space at the same time, and the transfer and distribution of energy according to the second law of thermodynamics. Microscopic causality appears to consist of certain restrictions imposed by one electron on the possible positions or states of another, and on the transfer of energy by electrons acquiring kinetic energy and losing it. What is the relation between these two concepts of 'occupation' and 'energy-transfer'? Since mass apparently occupies space, and since it is not now held that all mass is electrical, it is unlikely that the two concepts can be perfectly unified. Occupation of a certain position in space is not, however, prohibited only by the actual size of the electrons, etc., already occupying that region; these electrons are surrounded by fields, and one electron can occupy a certain position near another only if its energy is high enough. Thus occupation of space is partly a matter of energy—as we see on a macroscopic scale in the entry of a shell into an armour-plate (or even the occupation of a country by an aggressor nation!). When a set of objects is stationary, all the objects are in equilibrium with one another on the average. Thus in a gas the mean pressure on the walls of the vessel, due to the collisions of gas molecules with the walls, is on the average equal to the pressure exerted by the walls of the vessel. Now similar objects, or similar alterations, at the same point of space represent similar energies and have therefore no preference over one another. When, therefore, they come so close as to compete with one another for a certain position, neither can win, since neither has the requisite excess of energy. Thus if two volumes of gas at equal pressure are mixed, each molecule of one volume finds the other volume to be, on the average, occupied; it cannot move into the other volume and stay there permanently unless a molecule from the other gas comes out to make 'room' for it; for their mean energies are equal. On the other hand, if the added volume of gas is at a higher pressure, it finds the space of the first volume not fully occupied, since the mean kinetic energy of the second volume of gas is higher, and it will diffuse into the first space until equilibrium is restored. Thus, transfer of energy suggests a second kind of occupation of space, in which actual 'dimensions' of objects are replaced by their energies. Two things having equal energies cannot exist at the same place at the same time. Space here fulfils the function of bringing their energies into conflict, so to speak. For two objects repelling each other with a force varying as the fourth power of the distance between them, and in the field of many other such bodies at various distances, will find certain positions where they are in equilibrium, but any change of position would require more energy than either possesses, and so is impossible. When movement does occur in accordance with the second law of thermodynamics, it means of course that the total energy has become differently distributed, but is the same in amount as before. Thus, after an explosion the potential energy of the valency electrons, etc. has been changed into kinetic energy of molecules. It may be asked how potential energy can exist at all; perhaps one may suggest, as a speculation, that since energy has not fixed direction it is possible for two energies at one moment to oppose one another, and so be without visible or kinetic effect, and at another to assist each other in producing macroscopic movement, just as two steam-pipes issuing from a boiler might be joined in opposition, end to end, and would illustrate the existence of pressure and potential energy without motion or kinetic energy, whereas when the two ends are disconnected and laid open to the air, side by side, steam rushes from both, illustrating motion and kinetic energy.

But, it may be objected, how does the indication of some characteristic of a *concept* indicate anything about the nature of *objective reality*? This is related to Kant's fundamental problem—How can *a priori* synthetic propositions have objective validity?—and is part of the greater problem—How can any of our thoughts have objective validity? As mentioned before, Kant appears to shirk this issue, for he concludes that *a priori* synthetic propositions are valid only in regard to appearances, and not in regard to a transcendental object or the thing-in-itself. To be valid only of appearances is surely not true objective validity: the problem still remains—how, if at all, does our thinking manage to be valid in regard to objective reality, viz. physical objects? Now I am not arguing that the existence of an interactive factor in our concepts of objects puts a causal principle into reality, but the exact reverse—that our concepts of objects are derived from, and constructed to fit, reality, and therefore that they, and all the features they include when they 'fit the facts', are indicative of the nature of the pre-existing objective reality. Our concept represents the real object, and includes causal power as one of the real characteristics of objects. An attempt at further justification will be given in Chapters V, VI and VII.

The real justification of causality, however, must come from its trial by experiment; for, once we have admitted the possibility of symbolism in general (without which no speech or thought is possible) we must admit the possibility of symbols to represent alternatives, between which experiment may decide. If a certain type of symbolic formulation is so indefinite that it does not present the possibility of experimental solution, we must try some other kind.

The idea of causality does present very definite predictions as to events to be expected, provided suitable experimental precautions are taken; and, whatever modern theoretical physicists may say, most of the great hypotheses and experiments of Newton, Maxwell, Rutherford, Darwin and the rest have been inspired by the idea of tracing the action of causes in nature. Though we may never reach finality in seeking causes in between known causes and effects, the search is one which has always been rewarded, and the theory which prompts it deserves the credit. Nor is there any instance in which the idea of causality has led to false predictions; for the idea of causality in no way implies that we shall be able to observe all that is happening and predict with certainty in every case. On the other hand, the idea of causality will account in a general way for the anomalies and probabilities which we do find in experience; for a number of causes acting together—like the variations in charge in a cartridge, the play of wind on the bullet, the shaking of the marksman's arm, and so forth—will account for the slight variations in the position of the shots on a target. The only apparent objections to the idea of causality are surely derived from a falsely hypostatised view of it. Such are the objections to 'streaky' views of causality, or the attempt to designate objects definitely and finally as causes and effects. We are supporting the idea of causal interaction in nature, not of isolated and precise objects and events which may be labelled as causes or effects.

Again, we are admittedly unable to probe causation to the bottom and find ultimate links and a first cause; but this limitation on our thought—some possible reasons for which will be suggested in the following chapters—is no sufficient reason for rejecting the idea that reality may be constituted in this way. We should try out the idea as long as it works and suggests definite consequences.

So we may try to formulate a hypothesis concerning the nature of thought and reality, see whether any evidence at present available seems to support it, and wait to find whether the evidence gained in future gives any support to it or to slightly modified forms of it.

This experimental attitude has been well expressed by Helmholtz (vol. III, p. 532): 'The natural philosopher must stick to the facts and try to find out their laws; and he has no means of deciding between these two kinds of speculation, because materialism, it should be remembered, is just as much a metaphysical speculation or hypothesis as idealism, and therefore has no right to decide about matters of fact in natural philosophy except on a basis of facts. It is safer in my opinion to connect the phenomena of vision with other processes that are certainly present and actually effective, although they may require further explanation themselves, instead of trying to base these phenomena on perfectly unknown hypotheses as to the mechanism of the nervous system and the properties of nervous tissue, which have been invented for the purpose and have no analogy of any sort. The only justification I can see for proceeding in this way would be after all attempts had failed to explain the phenomena by known facts. But, in my judgment this is not the case at all with the physiological explanation of visual perception. On the contrary, the more attentively I have studied these phenomena, the more have I been impressed by the uniformity and harmony everywhere of the interplay of the psychic processes, and the more consistent and coherent this whole region of phenomena has appeared to me.'

It has been suggested—for instance by Bartlett—that an explanation, particularly in psychology, can be causal without being mechanistic, and that a mechanistic physical explanation often gives a more complicated rather than a simpler picture of the situation since its ultimate units—electrons, etc.—are so far removed from ordinary experience. Yet the advocate of physical explanations does not choose a mechanistic explanation gratuitously, or from prejudice, but is driven to it in his search for an adequate explanation or one which covers the most facts by the fewest postulates and leaves the fewest anomalies outstanding. This adequacy and freedom from anomalies is also the credential of the particles as being ultimate, remote as they may seem from everyday life. For, once rigid causality is admitted, whether it be thought to be mechanistic or not, anomalies must be regarded as cases where our explanatory concepts are wrong, and any modification which removes the anomalies and fits the facts is likely to be more correct. It is merely an empirical fact that these commendable modifications do, in practice, turn out to be along the lines of more and more physical explanation in the phenomena at present examined. Somewhere, consciousness enters and has its function; but the thought that this is so should not deter us from applying physical explanations as long as they reduce the anomalies. Indeed, we should find an increase in anomalies, or an increase in the number of facts which cannot be met, as soon as we apply physical explanations in spheres where they do not apply.

This plea for physical explanation does not mean that it is useless or incorrect to give apparently non-physical clinical explanations of psychological phenomena—for instance, to say that an unpleasant experience or shock may *cause* amnesia or suppression. This is a correct statement of the phenomena as far as it goes; but we are entitled to go further if we can. If we then find a more ultimate physical and physiological train of events to be involved 'in between' the shock and the suppression, we should regard this as a more ultimate part of the mechanism, just as it is correct to say that the pressure of one's finger on the self-starter causes the engine to go, but more fundamental to say that the pressure of one's finger causes current to flow in the windings of the starting motor and still more fundamental to give an account of the flow of current and torque exerted by the motor in terms of electronic and electro-magnetic theory.

CHAPTER V

Hypothesis on the nature of thought

FROM this point onwards we are advancing a hypothesis and shall take the existence of the external world and of causation for granted.

One of the most fundamental properties of thought is its power of predicting events. This gives it immense adaptive and constructive significance as noted by Dewey and other pragmatists. It enables us, for instance, to design bridges with a sufficient factor of safety instead of building them haphazard and waiting to see whether they collapse, and to predict consequences of recondite physical or chemical processes whose value may often be more theoretical than practical. In all these cases the process of thought, reduced to its simplest terms, is as follows: a man observes some external event or process and arrives at some 'conclusion' or 'prediction' expressed in words or numbers that 'mean' or refer to or describe some external event or process which comes to pass if the man's reasoning was correct. During the process of reasoning, he may also have availed himself of words or numbers. Here there are three essential processes:

(1) 'Translation' of external process into words, numbers or other symbols,

(2) Arrival at other symbols by a process of 'reasoning', deduction, inference, etc., and

(3) 'Retranslation' of these symbols into external processes (as in building a bridge to a design) or at least recognition of the correspondence between these symbols and external events (as in realising that a prediction is fulfilled).

One other point is clear; this process of reasoning has produced a final result similar to that which might have been reached by causing the actual physical processes to occur (e.g. building the bridge haphazard and measuring its strength or compounding certain chemicals and seeing what happened); but it is also clear that this is not what has happened; the man's mind does not contain a material bridge or the required chemicals. Surely, however, this process of prediction is not unique to minds, though no doubt it is hard to imitate the flexibility and versatility of mental prediction. A calculating machine, an anti-aircraft 'predictor', and Kelvin's tidal predictor all show the same ability. In all these latter cases, the physical process which it is desired to predict is *imitated* by some mechanical device or model which is cheaper, or quicker, or more convenient in operation. Here we have a very close parallel to our three stages of reasoning—the 'translation' of the external processes into their representatives (positions of gears, etc.) in the model; the arrival at other positions of gears, etc., by mechanical processes in the instrument; and finally, the retranslation of these into physical processes of the original type.

By a model we thus mean any physical or chemical system which has a similar relation-structure to that of the process it imitates. By 'relation-structure' I do not mean some obscure non-physical entity which attends the model, but the fact that it is a physical working model which works in the same way as the process it parallels, in the aspects under consideration at any moment. Thus, the model need not resemble the real object pictorially; Kelvin's tide-predictor, which consists of a number of pulleys on levers, does not resemble a tide in appearance, but it works in the same way in certain essential respects—it combines oscillations of various frequencies so as to produce an oscillation which closely resembles in amplitude at each moment the variation in tide level at any place. Again, since the physical object is 'translated' into a working model which gives a prediction which is retranslated into terms of the original object, we cannot say that the model invariably either precedes or succeeds the external object it models. The only logical distinction is on the ground of cheapness, speed, and convenience. The *Queen Mary* is designed with the aid of a model in a tank because of the greater cheapness and convenience of the latter; we do not design toy boats by trying out the different plans on boats the size of Atlantic liners. In the same way, in the particular case of our own nervous systems, the reason why I regard them as modelling the real process is that they permit trial of alternatives, in, e.g. bridge design, to proceed on a cheaper and smaller scale than if each bridge in turn were built and tried by sending a train over it, to see whether it was sufficiently strong.

Many mechanistic views of life and behaviour have been advanced, e.g. those of Hartley and Cabanis. But on the one hand there has been a tendency to *assert* a mechanistic theory rather than to regard it as a hypothesis which should, if followed out, indicate exactly how and where it breaks down; and on the other hand, there has been little attempt to formulate a definite plan of a mechanism which would fulfil the requirements. Hull has, however, made some models which show response to an altered stimulus, or conditioning. I have not committed myself to a definite picture of the mechanisms of synaptic resistance, facilitation, etc.; but I have tried, in the succeeding pages, to indicate what I suspect to be the fundamental feature of neural machinery—its power to parallel or model external events— and have emphasised the fundamental role of this process of paralleling in calculating machines. Thus, it is perhaps better to start with a definite idea as to the kind of tasks mechanism can accomplish in calculation, and the tasks it would have to accomplish in order to play a part in thought, rather than to draw analogies between the nervous system and some specific mechanism such as a telephone exchange and leave the matter there. A telephone exchange may resemble the nervous system in just the sense I think important; but the essential point is the principle underlying the similarity.

Now it may be that a mind does not function only in this way; but as this is *one* way that 'works', in fact the only way with which we are familiar in the physical sciences, and as there is abundant evidence of the great mechanical possibilities of the nervous system, it does not seem overbold to consider whether the brain does not work in this way— that it imitates or models external processes. The three processes of translation, inference, and retranslation then become the translation of external events into some kind of neural patterns by stimulation of the sense-organs, the interaction and stimulation of other neural patterns as in 'association', and the excitation by these of effectors or motor organs.

Without enquiring into the relation between such neural patterns and the unitary symbols of thought—words, numbers, etc.—we can study to some extent the scope and limits of this modelling or imitative process, by studying the scope and limits of the two great classes of symbols—words and numbers.

Any kind of working model of a process is, in a sense, an analogy. Being different it is bound somewhere to break down by showing properties not found in the process it imitates or by not possessing properties possessed by the process it imitates. Perhaps the extraordinary pervasiveness of number, and the multiplicity of operations which can be performed on number without leading to inconsistency, is not a proof of the 'real existence' of numbers as such but a proof of the extreme flexibility of the neural model or calculating machine. This flexibility renders a far greater number of operations possible for it than for any other single process or model.

Of course we have still to face the question *why* these analogies between different mechanisms—these similarities of relation-structure—should exist. To see common principles and simple rules running through such complexity is at first perplexing though intriguing. When, however, we find that the apparently complex objects around us are combinations of a few almost indestructible units, such as electrons, it becomes less perplexing. For it is inevitable that processes corresponding to arithmetical addition of these elementary units—electrons, protons, etc.—should manifest themselves in many instances. That is to say, if all pieces of pure iron consist of similar groupings of similar units, it is very likely that two pieces of iron placed end to end will add in length according to some simple law, and that pieces of other substances will do the same. The emergence of common principles and similarities is, then, not so surprising if it is shown that all substances are composed of similar ultimate units, for the appearance of uniformity and similarity is then the reappearance of a uniformity and similarity which were in fact ever present. We are still faced with the more ultimate question, why diverse materials should consist of combinations of a very few types of ultimate particles. The short life of some particles, such as positrons, suggests that in the vicinity of other particles, such as electrons, they are not stable; if it could be shown that in any such encounter the electron is more stable and the positron less, some kind of explanation would have been given as to why electrons are more frequent. It would still be conceivable that innumerable entirely different types of ultimate particle could have existed; if there is only one type in existence at a time there is nothing for it to be inconsistent with (apart from such factors as the mutual repulsion of similar particles and their consequent inability to form combinations). If, however, we conceive the world as made of a number of different types of ultimate unit, it is possible that they would prove to be mutually unstable and that all particles must acquire the same properties in order to exist, much as water in different tubes on a common arm always finds a constant level.

This, however, is very speculative; the point of interest for our present enquiry is that physical reality is built up, apparently, from a few fundamental types of units whose properties determine many of the properties of the most complicated phenomena, and this seems to afford a sufficient explanation of the emergence of analogies between mechanisms and similarities of relation-structure among these combinations without the necessity of any theory of objective universals.

We have now to enquire how the neural mechanism, in producing numerical measurement and calculation, has managed to function in a way so much more universal and flexible than any other. Our question, to emphasize it once again, is not to ask what kind of thing a number is, but to think what kind of mechanism could represent so many physically possible or impossible, and yet self-consistent, processes as number does.

The key may possibly lie in the following fact: in causal chains and physical or chemical combinations, the possibility of a given combination tends to be limited by other factors than the mere self-consistency of the combination. If you try to determine whether the series of integers can be extended to infinity by piling bricks on top of one another, you find that after a time the bricks fall down, or you cannot reach to pile any more up, or you run short of bricks or die; all these are extraneous difficulties. More subtle are the difficulties of adding nine oranges to nine apples, or of trying to produce a physical four-dimensional object. In all these cases we have not been satisfied with simply finding whether a given combination can exist along with other combinations; we have chosen a combination of combinations (i.e. a *number* of *objects*) which of course limits the number of possible self-consistent combinations, just as in a game of rolling balls into grooves under a glass lid the number of times all are simultaneously in their grooves decreases as the number of balls is increased. In a mechanism such as a telephone exchange or a nervous system, where one is not trying to produce new objects but merely combinations of active or excited elements, the possible combinations are at a maximum, limited only by remoteness of excited elements (*vide* failure of association) or decrease of excitation with time (*vide* forgetting). Even these difficulties can be to some extent overcome by further use of written and spoken symbols to act as a kind of reinforcing or relay system.

This greatly extended power is not unique to a mind; it could be illustrated by calculating machines. A machine working on a graphical principle might try to represent squaring and cubing by pointers moving along the x, y and z axes; it would inevitably come to a standstill or repeat itself when the volume of the cube equalled its own volume. On the other hand, a machine working on the principle of picking up gear-teeth by a repeated-multiplication process could go on raising any number to any power however large if it had sufficient dials on it.

It is likely then that the nervous system is in a fortunate position, as far as modelling physical processes is concerned, in that it has only to produce combinations of excited arcs, not physical objects; its 'answer' need only be a combination of consistent patterns of excitation—not a new object that is physically and chemically stable.

We have now to enquire what meaning causality, meaning, implication, consistency and so forth can have when applied to such a mechanism. Again, our question is not 'What kind of thing is implication or causality?' but 'What structure and processes are required in a mechanical system to enable it to imitate correctly and to predict external processes or create new things?'

In examining this question, we can divide the process of thinking or reasoning into the same steps as before—representation by symbols, calculation, and retranslation into events.

The diversity of calculating machines, languages and words for numbers shows that a relation can be represented in several symbolic ways. *Unique determination* is the main principle; a symbol, a setting of a machine, or a neural pattern is liable to be misleading if it represents two distinct types of physical things or events.

Causality in the external world would be represented by some (causal) process of interaction between excited elements in our own brains. As a result of such interactive or associative processes we might have, for example, $A = B$, $B = C$, $A \neq C$, where A, B and C are neural patterns claiming to represent external things or processes. These patterns clearly cannot all remain simultaneously excited; inconsistency means a clash in the interaction of patterns.

My hypothesis then is that thought models, or parallels, reality—that its essential feature is not 'the mind', 'the self', 'sense-data', nor propositions but symbolism, and that this symbolism is largely of the same kind as that which is familiar to us in mechanical devices which aid thought and calculation.

I hope no one will be deterred by the idea that such a theory regards thought as an inactive halo round mechanical brain processes; for though my hypothesis assumes that thought processes and consciousness are dependent on mechanical processes, it tries to discover what function consciousness does perform, by seeing where a purely mechanical process fails to meet the facts. As will be discussed in Chapter VI, if it is true, it would be a hylozoistic rather than a materialistic scheme; it would attribute consciousness and conscious organisation to matter when it is physically organised in certain ways. However, these are remote speculations; the important point is to propound the theory and to consider ways of testing it.

We shall not consider purely speculative consequences of it, but only inferences which have some possibility of being experimentally verified, though we cannot claim that they provide critical tests of it. There remains the vitalist possibility—that life and mind, something different and aloof from physical matter, enters, and that we are misguided in our attempts to explain any aspects of conscious processes in terms of their material basis. But if so, the failure ought to show itself somewhere, if we proceed with due caution in the proposal and testing of hypotheses.

It is generally agreed that thought employs symbols such as written or spoken words or tokens; but it is not generally considered whether the whole of thought may not consist of a process of symbolism, nor is the nature of symbolism and its presence or absence in the inorganic world discussed. Further, it has been usual to restrict the word 'symbol' to words or tokens, which still leaves the processes of the relating of words to form sentences and the processes of inference and implication mysterious and unique. Let us consider whether these processes are not paralleled by familiar mechanisms.

First, we have seen that the possibility of verbal or other symbolism is the fundamental assumption of all philosophy communicated by anyone to anyone else. Without falling into the trap of attempting a precise definition, we may suggest a theory as to the general nature of symbolism, viz.

that it is the ability of processes to parallel or imitate each other, or the fact that they can do so since there are recurrent patterns in reality. The concepts of abilities and patterns and formal identity in material diversity are all hard ones; but the point is that symbolism does occur, and that we wish to explore its possibilities. There are three main steps: first, is there any evidence of such symbolism in inorganic nature? secondly, do we ourselves employ such symbolism in thought? and thirdly, is there any evidence that our thought processes themselves involve such symbolism, occurring within our brains and nervous systems?

There are plenty of instances in nature of processes which parallel each other—the emptying of pools and the discharge of a cat's fur which has become electrified, the transmission of sound and electromagnetic and ocean waves, and so forth. As mentioned above, human thought has a definite function; it provides a convenient small-scale model of a process so that we can, for instance, design a bridge in our minds and know that it will bear a train passing over it instead of having to conduct a number of full-scale experiments; and the thinking of animals represents on a more restricted scale the ability to represent, say, danger before it comes and leads to avoidance instead of repeated bitter experience. In inorganic nature, because of its simpler organisation, we should expect this function to be less fully exemplified. Indeed, there are very few examples at all. Perhaps the nearest approach is the fine trickle of water which first finds its way from a mountain spring down to the sea and smoothes a little channel for the greater volume of water which follows after it. But the *material* of symbolism— the parallel mechanisms—seem to be there; it is only the sensitive 'receptors' on matter, and means of intercommunication or nervous system, which are lacking.

Again, there is no doubt that we do use external and

mechanical symbolisation to assist our own thinking. Provided with a piece of paper we can perform long and complicated calculations which would be impossible in our heads; and the Busch differential analyser will solve problems which could not be tackled by any other method.

Finally, there is some, though scanty, evidence from anatomy and electrophysiology that our nervous systems do contain conducting sensory and motor paths and synapses in which there occur states of excitation and volleys of impulses which parallel the stimuli which occasioned them; so that, as far as experimental evidence goes, this symbolisation is found to occur in the central nervous system. But what produces and occasions it, on such a mechanistic theory? In any mechanical system, the events which occur are those which result in the greatest possible equalisation of energy—roughly speaking, the reactions take the path of least resistance. If parts of an organisation are interconnected by a system of communication such as the nervous system, the reactions can be directed along the 'lines of least resistance' by the expenditure of a very little energy in the appropriate 'lines of least resistance' in the nervous system. The situation is enormously complicated by natural selection, which causes the survival of certain organisms—those, for instance, in whom the passage of the 'monitoring' nerve impulse results in such activity of the whole organism as will tend to preserve it. In general, it is much more illuminating to regard the growth of symbolising power from this aspect of survival-value, rather than from the purely physical side of accordance with thermodynamics; but it does not seem that there is any inconsistency between the two.

Thus there are instances of symbolisation in nature; we use such instances as an aid to thinking; there is evidence of similar mechanisms at work in our own sensory and

central nervous systems; and the function of such symbolisa-
sation is plain. If the organism carries a 'small-scale model'
of external reality and of its own possible actions within
its head, it is able to try out various alternatives, conclude
which is the best of them, react to future situations before
they arise, utilise the knowledge of past events in dealing
with the present and future, and in every way to react in
a much fuller, safer, and more competent manner to the
emergencies which face it. Most of the greatest advances
of modern technology have been instruments which extended
the scope of our sense-organs, our brains or our limbs. Such
are telescopes and microscopes, wireless, calculating machines,
typewriters, motor cars, ships and aeroplanes. Is it not
possible, therefore, that our brains themselves utilise comparable mechanisms to achieve the same ends and that these
mechanisms can parallel phenomena in the external world
as a calculating machine can parallel the development of
strains in a bridge?

CHAPTER VI

Some consequences of this hypothesis

A HYPOTHESIS is usually advanced after an inductive survey of the facts which it has to explain. It can then be tested by the agreement or disagreement of predictions based on it with new facts which are discovered and its merits assessed by the degree of modification which it requires in order to meet these new facts. Thus before the details of a possible mechanism of thought are suggested, we must consider the facts—the subtlety, the extreme elasticity and modifiability of thought and behaviour, the importance of thought which does not issue in action and the function of consciousness or conscious processes.

It is in accordance with the theory of knowledge which we have supported that fact and theory should be inextricably bound and that each particular piece of knowledge should be justified only by its consistency with the rest of the system. In the hope of suggesting such a system for the facts and theories of psychology and physiology I shall therefore review observations and suggest tentative hypotheses without much distinction and can only ask for lenience and the test of future experiment. I am not claiming at any point to have 'explained away' any of these psychological facts, but only to suggest their relations and linkages with other facts or fruitful hypotheses in other fields of knowledge in the hope that something may be gained from the coordination of the two and from experiments based upon this idea.

On this theory meaning and implication would have a definite significance. 'Meaning', as we shall mention in the next chapter, appears to be used in two senses—general meaning or meaningfulness, which would be the power of words to symbolise things and events through the neural events which parallel those things and give rise to words and images. Meaning is also used in ordinary language in a particular sense to signify the object referred to by a certain word: this, then, is the particular reference or symbolism involved.

'Implication' would be the power of these neural mechanisms to operate on each other as the real events act causally on each other, so that the words or other symbols arouse each other as the real events produce each other. Implication would thus be a kind of artificial causation in which symbols connected by rules represent events connected by causal interaction—much as a war-game conducted according to rules might represent a real engagement in which the result was determined by the numbers, resources and strategy of the combatants. Language, in which sounds or written symbols represent things and actions, is one example of such a system; money, which represents labour, is another.

Recognition, again, has its mechanical analogies. A machine can, in a sense, 'recognise' or give the same internal or overt response to an event on successive occasions. Men and indicating instruments are both capable of this. There are, however, two striking differences between the type of 'recognition' most easy for man and for machine. For a man and for animals recognition of an absolute magnitude—the brightness of a light, the loudness of a sound, or the size of an angle—is extraordinarily difficult, whereas the recognition of a common relation (e.g. A is larger than a and B is larger than b) is relatively easy. This is shown in many of Lashley's (1938) experiments. Again, recognition of the shape of an object is made no harder, for man, by its presentation on slightly different parts of the retina, on the retina of the other eye, or at a somewhat unusual angle. An indicating instrument, on the other hand, usually requires the quantity which it measures to be applied in a quite stereotyped and rigid manner.

These differences may indicate a fundamental difference between recognition in its physical and psychological senses; on the other hand, they may only show that a different form of mechanism is involved in psychological recognition. Even what is known of the physiology of the senses shows that they are ill-equipped to act as reliable and constant indicators of absolute magnitudes; for instance, adaptation to constant stimulation occurs, and there is interaction between one or more sense-organs or parts of the same sense-organ, simultaneously stimulated. It would not be difficult to construct an electrical model of the eye which would show high sensitivity to slight differences in simultaneously or successively presented illuminations, provided that the spatial or temporal interval between them was not too great, but which would be remarkably insensitive to absolute values of illumination. Such a model would involve differentiating condensers whose operation bears a close analogy to the action of sensory adaptation and to the evanescent nature of the 'memory traces' of absolute sensory intensities. Thus we see sufficient reasons, in the operation of the sense-organs, why recognition of absolute intensities should be difficult. But we have yet to understand why the appreciation and recognition of relative size and brightness, or of the identity of figures imaged on different parts of the retina, should be easy.

As Lashley remarks, mere lack of discrimination in the response of an animal may give its behaviour a false appearance of generalisation and abstraction. I am not sure, however, that the appearance is necessarily false. It may be that in genuine generalisation apparently abstract properties of objects are really recognised as the same because, acting on the brain mechanisms of the animal, they produce the same effect, just as a pound of butter and a pound of bacon both produce the same deflection on a balance. In other words, the brain mechanism of the rat may really pick out number-of-corners or relative-nearness-of-right-hand-corner-to-margin as 'tangible' features, and disregard absolute size and absolute retinal position (the things to which an ordinary mechanical device would react so easily) not because it 'transcends' these simple characteristics but because they are actually *harder* for it to recognise.[1] Our problem, then, is to consider what kind of mechanical device could respond more easily to these apparently high-grade relational characteristics, presented in a fluid manner, than to more rigid data. Adaptation, and probably the fluidity of the 'traces', if there are such things, representing absolute intensities would account for the difficulty of recognising absolute intensities. Adaptation will also, to some extent, explain the ease of recognising relative equality or relative difference between pairs of stimuli. It is very little easier to recognise, after the lapse of time, a difference in physical brightness of 50% than an absolute brightness of 100 e.f.c. On the other hand, we can hardly forget that two brightnesses which are different are so. There are now fewer alternatives to confuse us; we have only to recognise the sameness or the difference of the brightness of two lights; we need not 'place' it at a particular point in a scale of innumerable brightnesses. (There is evidence that forgetting is sometimes a function of the number of alternatives available—and that this is a factor in the difficulty of remembering arbitrary numbers or arbitrary directions, as compared with logical

[1] Since the above was written Lashley (1941) has emphasised that generalisation may indeed be a rather elementary power of nervous tissue.

material where, in ways that we cannot consider at the moment, our previous formulations and ideas limit the number of alternatives that can be seriously considered.) Adaptation seems to 'differentiate' in the mathematical sense; it abstracts changes from absolute intensities, and confers on them a definiteness, and a position where there is less confusion and ambiguity.

Differentiation, then, is a process by which ordinary absolute quantities and constants vanish and rates of change take their place as absolute quantities. Such reification of change must be based on a *series* of data in space or time. It is impossible to differentiate a single point in space with regard to anything.

Differentiation can be achieved electrically by a condenser and resistance system. The essential feature of this arrangement is that, at every moment, it starts off from zero, where that zero represents the condition at the preceding moment. If we apply a steady voltage to such a system it will be represented, after a very short interval, by zero volts; and if we increase this voltage by 1 volt per second, this will show as an absolute voltage of 1. Such a resistance–condenser system can never be mathematically perfect, but it can discriminate between the time courses of events so that very slow ones are not indicated, and rapid alterations alone recorded; this selective action is of course due to the time constant of the system.

The apprehension of the similarity of two curves despite differences in their size or position is another type of abstraction less easy to understand. Sometimes, indeed, it is exactly equivalent to mathematical differentiation. Constants shift the position of a curve, and constants disappear in differentiation. This does not tell us *how* this abstraction or differentiation is achieved, any more than the occurrence of 'differentiation' or intensity in the eye tells us *how* it is achieved; we must work out the photochemical and neural mechanisms of adaptation on their own score; but it is interesting to consider the part they play in behaviour. In the same way we can classify the recognition of bends and angles, irrespective of the size of the total figure and its retinal location, as an example of the differentiation of the figure, by which the absolute figure vanishes, and the angles and relative characteristics become the absolute characteristics. But we must consider by what mechanism this can be achieved.

Can we conceive anything equivalent to this 'sieve', the time constant, which lets absolute magnitudes and positions in space, instead of in time, run through, while retaining the alterations of direction and the bends?

One difficulty is that time is unidirectional and has only one dimension, while space has three. It is not clear, at first, whether we want some kind of differentiation relatively to *position* or to *direction* in space.

It is fairly clear that integration irrespective of direction would be meaningless; for if the direction by reference to which differentiation were accomplished changed randomly from spot to spot and from moment to moment (which comes to the same thing), even a straight line would have an infinite variety of simultaneous solutions. On the other hand, our ability to recognise figures at various angles, and even to interpret them in different ways (e.g. ambiguous figures), indicates that differentiation is possible in a multitude of directions, determined mainly by the figure itself. This suggests that summation occurs over a small length of a straight line, and determines the direction of differentiation. Probably the same mechanism is at work in the case of vernier acuity, where a lateral shift of one part of a line is detectable even though it represents an angular shift of only about 10 seconds, if the length of the lines themselves exceeds a certain minimum. We must, then, consider how the nervous system might achieve two essential steps in the process:

(1) The summation of several points of stimulation, lying on a straight line, so as to give rise to a state of neural excitation or trace or pattern having *direction*, which may be called a 'vector element'; and

(2) How differentiation occurs, so that a series or line of such vector elements having the same direction possesses little or no perceptual significance, whereas a bend or discontinuity in it has a very marked one.

The easiest mechanical or electrical method would be to make a 'visual cortex' in which every point of the retina is projected in exactly the same position, relative to every other point, as in the retina, and to use a dioptric system such that straight lines in the physical object are represented by straight lines in the retina image. Some 'over-shooting' mechanism might then be arranged, by which a mechanical or electrical impulse having some inertia travels from each stimulated point to the next; it will then be brought up with a jerk if it runs along a line of stimulated points and suddenly reaches its end, or a bend in the line. However, as there is evidence against the existence of such point-to-point projection of the retina (e.g. the diffuse loss of vision resulting from cortical lesions), and as the dioptric system certainly does not project physically straight lines as straight on the retina, we must envisage some more generalised mechanism, and in the present state of physiological and anatomical knowledge it may appear fruitless to make more detailed hypotheses here.

This may be one of the functions of consciousness—to permit a greater 'elasticity' and flexibility and unity of response than the known properties of co-ordinations of mechanisms will accomplish.

Let us consider the conditions in more detail.

ABSTRACTION AND BRAIN MECHANISMS

As remarked above one of the characteristics of memory and perception is the recognition of identity or of similarity. To recognise a thing is surely to react to it, internally or overtly, as the 'same thing' to which we reacted on a previous occasion.

In the above sense mechanical devices can show some degree of recognition. A photocell can respond in the same way to apples having the same colour, a penny-in-the-slot machine to similar coins, and so forth. Men and animals are capable of this, but of much more. The progressive stages of recognition may be classified as:

(1) Those in which all the conditions of stimulation are identical, within the limits of discrimination of the organism;

(2) Those in which there are differences in the peripheral stimulation, but in which these may be 'corrected' by other sensory impulses so as to lead to the production of an identical pattern of central stimulation;

(3) Those in which such correction is inadequate or lacking, so that there are points of difference between the stimulation on two occasions, these points of difference being perceptible by the organism, yet the thing is recognised as the same in certain important aspects; and

(4) Those in which the differences extend to all direct sensory qualities and physical constituents, so that the sameness of the two objects is confined to some abstract characteristic such as triangularity, number, and other spatial or temporal relations or vague qualities such as intellectual difficulty.

How should we set about designing a mechanism to respond to these different kinds of identity, and identity in diversity?

A mechanical device is sensitive if any energy reaching it makes a relatively large alteration in its form or kinetic energy or position. Thus, a small amount of energy reaching an explosive causes a large alteration in its condition or form; a little energy reaching the lid of a jack-in-a-box makes a large alteration in its shape and position; and a little energy reaching a galvanometer or voltmeter makes a large alteration in the position of the spot of light or the pointer.

Any mechanical device which is sensitive will give the same response (within the limits of its random error) to two identical situations, i.e. two identical amounts of energy, reaching it in the same form and under the same conditions, if the instrument itself is unaltered. This appears to me an elementary form of recognition. (An instrument, like an animal, can respond differently to the same immediate situation if it itself is altered. An animal responds differently to food if it is hungry or satisfied, my typewriter responds differently to pressure on a letter-key according to whether the shift-key is depressed or not, and a wireless set responds differently to an identical signal according to whether its battery is fresh or nearly run down.) Let us first consider the cases of the *same* reaction to situations which are, in some respect, the same.

A machine may contain some correcting system which transforms different types of 'peripheral' stimulation into identical stimulation further up, and thus gives a 'recognition response'. Thus a temperature-compensated aneroid barometer may give the same pointer reading in response to identical barometric pressures though the degree of expansion of the metal chamber may be different in the two cases, owing to a difference in atmospheric temperature. This behaviour has many analogies in the realm of human recognition, e.g. in the distinction between real and apparent movement of objects when the ocular muscles are active or paralysed, or in the case of visual adaptation to different illuminations. No doubt the compensation is often more flexible and more affected by its success or failure in the human being, but in essentials the mechanism would seem analogous.

Next, we have the case where, even after all corrections, the two situations are not similar throughout, but only in parts, and the identity of these parts is recognised. In simple cases, this also can be done by a machine; in fact, it is the commonest occurrence, since most indicators are only sensitive to one 'aspect' of an object—its temperature, its weight, its voltage, its colour and so forth. Thus, a balance 'recognises' a weight of 1 gram, whether it be the weight of a piece of brass or of lead. In the same way we can recognise colours apart from the nature of the coloured objects. There is thus nothing very mysterious about the recognition of 'identity in diversity'.

Finally come the more subtle forms of recognition—recognition of similar shapes of different sizes, or casting their images on different parts of the retina, of the 'three-ness' of three apples or three oranges, or of relations such as 'to the left of'. These represent degrees of 'abstraction', that is, separation of the common characteristic from any particular physical object or situation, and of 'relation', that is, of position in space and time relatively to other objects.

Sometimes a simple mechanical device will show this power in a high degree. Thus, an inclined plane will 'recognise' spheres, of whatever size, material and colour, and 'distinguish' them from cubes, since the former will roll down it while the latter will not. But we must not underestimate the extreme flexibility and adaptability of the mechanism of recognition in man and animals on account of a few specific and special mechanisms of this kind.

'Abstraction' in itself offers little difficulty. A photoelectric counter may count objects of very varied nature; it relies only on their passage along a conveyer belt with intervals between them. Surely it is, in a sense, actuated by 'number' in the abstract. .

The recognition of spatial and temporal relations begins to offer greater difficulties, and suggests the great flexibility which characterises recognition in men and animals. Here there is quite definitely something which is common to the two situations which are recognised as similar, or in some respect identical, but it is a very subtle something—triangularity, for instance. All mechanical recognition which we have discussed above consists in the identical response of an instrument to a situation, or to some part of that situation to which it is sensitive. In the same way, we must now consider either what kind of mechanism would be sufficiently flexible to respond similarly to triangles of different sizes and retinal locations, *or* we have to consider what kind of corrective mechanism could transform these different types of peripheral stimulation into 'invariants' to which some central mechanism would give identical responses. That is to say, we may thrust the burden of making recognition possible either on the detector mechanism or on the corrective mechanism. In all cases of 'recognition' by instruments which we have considered, the final response consists in the actuation of some single part of the instrument in the same way by both sets of conditions; that is, there is convergence of stimulation on the final indicator. If a mechanical theory of recognition is to cope with the recognition of triangularity, I think some similar convergent device must be postulated, so that the triangles, whatever their size and retinal location, finally excite some common neural pattern which represents their triangularity. The burden would rest on the mechanism which causes the retinal images of the different images to excite this common pattern. This would, I think, involve the abstraction of the geometrical determinants of the figure—the *angles*, and their *three-ness*. It may be complained that children recognise figures without being able to specify the geometrical features which they have in common, and that adults are often unconscious of the geometrical relations which enable them to recognise a face or a piece of furniture. But this unconsciousness no more disproves the reality of those processes than our unconsciousness of the innervation of our arm muscles disproves the existence of neural transmission and muscular contraction. Nor are we claiming that recognition involves unconscious response to *all* the geometrical features of an object; the response may well be based on a few of the simpler ones and will only be made more selective if mistakes occur.

What kind of mechanism, then, can we conceive as being capable of abstracting the angles of a triangle and their number? The recognition of number, again, is the least difficult part of the process. Once we have a definite, unitary, neural process representing a corner or an angle of a certain size, the response to the number of such angles is equivalent to the response of the photoelectric counter. The difficulty is in seeing how anything so variable and elastic as the image of an angle, falling on any part of the retina, comes to be represented by a specific neural process. In the same way, we can represent an angle, wherever its image falls on our retina, by a number of teeth on a wheel in a calculating machine; and once such symbolic representation is accomplished, the calculating machine can do the rest—can tell us the relation of that angle to others, and its identity with an angle that we represented on the machine the week before. The hardest part of the process is the act of representation itself—the representation of something variable in size and location by a definite neural process.

Every physical property is relative to a certain context; thus a voltage must be measured relatively to another voltage. Even absolute zero and other natural fixed points depend on other standards which are taken for granted. In the same way, an angle is a property of a line of points relative to each other—the property that the points around any one point proceed in certain directions with regard to it. This dependence of spatial characteristics, such as angularity, on the relation of points to one another in space is difficult and confusing. We could, however, make an absolute detector of angles. For instance, a scanning beam in a Zworykin electron camera could be passed over a few points on a straight line and could be caused, by the current it picked up from each illuminated spot on a straight line, to bend itself so as to pass along the direction of the first few points on the line. It would then change its direction by a standard amount, for a given angle, whatever the position of this angle on the screen; and the change of direction could be indicated (by condenser coupling) as an absolute change in voltage on the beam deflector plates. The essential thing about any such device is that it must respond to straightness and to bentness; and the simplest device for doing this is some device which acquires a 'habit' in passing along the straight part of the line, and consequently encounters a break when it is faced by something new. In other words, if a machine is to appreciate a relation, the different related things must be blended into a single response, so that any new stimulus will fall within, or contradict, that response. In the case of the visual cortex, the excitation of points representing a more or less straight line on the retina must cause some single response, and the excitation of other points not on this line a different response. Further, we must remember that this is accomplished not merely for three angles but for the whole spatial framework of the visual field; and that it is accomplished by an apparently random mass of nerve fibres. This, however, may really simplify the problem; for it means that the state of excitation may be almost the same in the two regions of the visual cortex, if the sizes of the images are the same, and may be similar if they differ in size. Now if every neurone in that stimulated pattern bears a certain average relation to every other, it is possible that some fairly simple characteristic of the whole pattern— for instance, the excitation travelling down a few neurones which lead away from it to some other visual area—is uniquely determined by that particular visual pattern. In the same way, if the fluid pressure at perhaps half a dozen points within an ocean wave were measured, it might be found that no form of surface other than that of the actual wave would cause the pressure at those points to be just what it is. It is thus conceivable that a highly complicated pattern of local stimulation may make a fairly simple 'label' or symbol for itself, in the form of a pattern of stimulation travelling to a common centre.[1]

Measurement is a form of symbolisation. It consists in assigning numerals to objects or quantities with a view to obtaining objectively valid results from arithmetical calculations with these numerals. It therefore has three interesting features: first, the assignation of numerals is a type of symbolisation; secondly, the calculation involves functional symbolism, rules similar to the rules of implication, followed by retranslation of the results obtained into material terms when necessary; and thirdly, this type of numerical symbolism has a greater degree of generality than any other— almost everything in the world can be represented by a

[1] Since the above was written Lashley (1941) has proposed a theory of interference patterns in the brain which is in some ways similar to the above. I still feel, however, that some more permanent pattern, dependent possibly on synaptic resistance, though not dependent on a particular set of nerve fibres, must be postulated to account for memory.

number and can be measured in some respect. We have suggested that this extreme generality and utility of number is assisted by the mechanism of the nervous system, which may enable a similar response of enumeration or estimation to be applied to anything which stimulates it at all, and, like a calculating machine, can itself model or imitate more mathematical operations with these quantities than most physical processes.

It may be objected that we cannot conceive any possible neural correlate of the concept of a number, and that a neural calculating machine would, in fact, never give rise to or employ such concepts; its working would be a continuous and unconscious process. Hypostatisation, naming, and the employment of concepts and images in thought may thus be taken as an argument against our theory.

Yet it is clear that, when any calculating machine is in operation, there are objects or events—the number of teeth projecting from an Odner wheel or the radial distance of the friction wheel on an integrating disc—which represent numbers, and that, to the man who observes the machine, these have a greater degree of 'thinghood' and conceptual definiteness than the interconnecting parts and the continuous transmission of motion from one part to another. In the same way in a neural calculating machine there may well be patterns of excitation in the cortex, temporal and spatial groupings of impulses, and so forth which, to a physiologist sufficiently skilled, would 'represent' concepts or sensations of objects. Admittedly, there is a large gap between postulating that such patterns might be interpreted, by another physiologist, as representing images and postulating that they give rise, in the possessor of that brain, to images; but there is no evidence against the idea. Just as a railway system consists of communicating lines on which trains are in continuous motion and stations where they stop and where definite events—such as the growth of factories—tend to occur, so there may be patterns of excitation or moments in a series of impulses at which there is some kind of demarcation which issues into consciousness as an image. Some parts of the process of neural transmission from sensory receptor to motor organ may have a physiological definiteness which is correlated with their psychological definiteness or emergence into consciousness as images.

This concept of 'thinghood' is of fundamental importance for any theory of thought. In proposing any such theory we are faced with a momentous choice: Are we to say, with Butler, that 'everything is what it is and not another thing', and insist that images, thoughts, concepts, the self, and all these other reifications and hypostatisations are undeniable realities, and consequently to reject any explanation of them in terms of other processes? Or are we to suggest that everything is not always what it seems at first sight to be and claim the right to see whether some other explanation or some other mechanism will not account for the facts as we know them in a satisfactory manner? We have given some reasons for choosing the second alternative. We have tried to show that this hypostatisation of the self, of thought, images, sense-data and so forth is a kind of naïve realism of the world of consciousness which, like naïve realism in regard to perception of the external world, does not work—that it depends on the assertion of the undeniable truth of particular observations and introspections and interpretations of single events and that it leads to inconsistency and suggests no hypothesis which can be subjected to test.

We commonly apply names and the concept of thinghood to those assemblages of particles in the external world which are composed of molecules of the same kind, have similar properties, regular boundaries, lasting existence, influence on their surroundings and so forth. These are 'cues' of thinghood just as there are cues in the perception of distance (convergence, accommodation, height of base of object in visual field, known size of object, etc.). Such cues are certainly operative in our apparently direct perceptual judgment, though it has been argued for many years whether one should describe this process of utilisation as subconscious interpretation or in some other way.

It is often stated glibly that the whole is greater than the sum of its parts. What exactly is meant by this? It is contended that the whole has properties which are novel and which could not be predicted from a knowledge of the parts. It is implied, I suppose, that two or more elements may combine in a way which is unique and without precedent, so that prediction of the result is impossible. But in actual fact things combine according to laws which are not unique; the particular combination may be unique and without precedent, but the steps which have given rise to it are orderly and determined by the discoverable properties of its constituents; and the result may be not without analogy in other events known to us. Thus, although we have no word which describes uniquely the particular ink blot I may make by shaking my pen, unique in detail and unrepeatable in all time, still we have words for that kind of object and can predict the kind of way in which it will behave—will spread, dry, fade, etc. But we can go further than this; we can combine words so as to describe the spatial arrangements and peculiar properties of that drop. In short, where things can go, words can follow, and can even go ahead. For we use a language and a logic derived from the observation of objects and their behaviour, and so arranged that words and the rules for their combination and usage give them all the properties of objects for any given purpose. Objects act causally on one

another; words can be made to imply other words, by the
rules of implication, themselves founded on the rules of
causality which govern material things. It thus becomes
possible, by using words in accordance with these rules of
implication, to forestall the development of material events,
and so to predict them. If a verbal formula fails to describe
a future event correctly, either the words are too narrow
and incomplete in their description of the properties of the
constituent atoms, or the mind of the scientist fails to combine them as the causal sequence would combine the real
objects. Errors can thus occur, but their occurrence does
not render the prediction of new combinations and properties impossible. Again, it seems often to be held that the
prediction of the behaviour of a multitude of atoms in
combination can easily foretell their combined actions being
more complicated than that of the atoms themselves, but
cannot foresee their action in combination being simpler,
and so fails to predict new units or wholes. This seems to me
untrue. Calculation of the combined apparent movements
of the planets has led to the concept of their simple rotation
round the sun, and of the invention of the phrase 'solar
system' to describe this whole, even though no one has
ever stood at some distant point in space, normal to the
ecliptic, from which he might see that system as an obvious
unit or pattern. Nor is anyone's span of apprehension
sufficient to see the actual movement of the planets in their
orbits. The fact that so great a whole as the solar system has
been conceived and visualised simply from a consideration
of its parts, seems to me to belie the suggestion that the
whole is greater than the sum of its parts in any sense which
would imply the futility of seeking an explanation of the
behaviour of the whole in terms of the nature and behaviour
of the parts. Of course it is still legitimate to employ some
large-scale calculus such as statistics or chemistry or relativity

to relate certain highly integrated wholes whose detailed prediction in terms of constituents would be too laborious to be possible. But explanation in terms of constituents and their combinations still remains the ultimate type of explanation and the type to which all relational explanation must return whenever faced with some anomaly or when asked to say whether some phenomenon, such as life or consciousness, involves an entirely new entrant or vital principle, not to be found in or constructed by the combination of physical atoms.

I have not tried to show that a whole is *never* greater than the sum of its parts, but to show that in many cases where the whole appears to have new properties these properties in fact arise from, and are predictable in terms of, the properties of the parts. Thus one should not assume too readily that combination into wholes introduces such complete novelty that science cannot predict the new properties that appear.

If we start from the other side of the problem, we may say that reality—physical and mental—appears to consist of arrangements of material units and of units of energy. Some of these arrangements are atoms. Further arrangements of these arrangements are possible, often through the agency of catalysts and enzymes and produce crystals, liquids, powders, etc.; whenever there is a high concentration in a particular place of arrangements of arrangements (e.g. a lump composed of one kind of atom), we have one kind of organisation; and such organisations tend to have more marked effects on their environments than unconcentrated or unorganised arrangements of arrangements. This phenomenon is the beginning, perhaps, of the division of matter into less organised parts, such as soil, and more organised parts, such as rivers and animals. It can occur in the course of nature just as if a number of powdered chemicals came into contact; at most points mere physical mixture would occur, without startling results; but at some places chemicals capable of combination would meet and perhaps produce explosives which would be very much more active and far-reaching in their effects, perhaps blowing all the rest of the mixture and its surroundings into fragments. I do not mean that concentration of one kind of arrangement is the only kind or the chief kind of organisation; it is perhaps a first essential; but the sea and the soil fulfil this requirement fairly well and yet are not highly organised. Concentration in such a way as to give continuity of form, unidirection of energy, and finally the combination of different types of organisation to provide further versatility and adaptability of form and of movement and effect are necessary. Investigation along these aetiological lines might help to solve Braithwaite's puzzle—that wholes are ordinarily sets in which the parts reciprocally determine one another; and yet that Gestalt wholes, such as drawn figures, do not necessarily show any causal interdependence of their parts at all (except through the observing mind and brain).

It seems, then, that language must try to suit itself to the description of these more and more highly organised arrangements, having ill-defined limits in many cases, and capable of emerging from the most unpromising material and of exhibiting the most surprising properties. We shall try later to show in more detail how this may be done.

But language has a more important function than such mere description. It must evolve rules of implication governing the use of words, in such a way that a line of thought can run parallel to, and predict, causally determined events in the external world. The ability of a particular 'line of thought' to do this is the test of its correctness as an explanation; if it is successful, it 'works'—it 'covers' the facts. Some may object that this reduces thought to a mere 'copy' of reality and that we ought not to want such an internal 'copy'; are not electrons, causally interacting, good enough? Why do we want our minds to play the same sort of game, with laws of implication instead of causal laws to determine the next step? The answer, I think, is first, that only this internal model of reality—this working model— enables us to predict events which have not yet occurred in the physical world, a process which saves time, expense, and even life. Secondly, the highly accurate and efficient interaction of electrons does not tell us what we want to know; it is a machine which works very well, but we only see the outside of it; and if we wish to find how many inter- mediate steps are involved—how many parts and operations there are in the machine—we have to reconstruct it in terms of implicative laws between logical entities in our minds. For the machine works equally well whether we are ignorant of certain causal steps in it or not; but scientific thought does not work equally well if there is a gap in the chain somewhere; we shall find ourselves faced with obstacles to thought and inconsistency between data if there are any missing or faulty links. (But of course language, its terms, and its laws of implication, may lead to misdescription of bodies and their causal behaviour; then it becomes mis- leading, and linguistic difficulties are falsely thought to in- dicate paradoxes and mysteries in external reality.) This working model in our minds, besides elucidating the causal steps of a process, can prescribe the characteristics necessary for the 'elements', more or less ultimate, which it is using as a means of explanation; and so it might be relevant to the problem whether, for instance, life entails a 'new entrant'—a different kind of fundamental element—from those which suffice to explain the behaviour of non-living matter, or whether, on the contrary, all the phenomena of life result from highly organised rearrangements of these elements. Some new attribute of the material elements may have to be postulated to account for consciousness; but this would not be the same as postulating an entirely new entrant, independent of matter for its thought and behaviour.

Further, if satisfactory thought consists of the working of such a model of reality, we can answer, to a great extent, the problem of emergent evolution—the problem of whether the arrangements of elements can lead to wholes and types of behaviour which could not have been predicted from knowledge of the behaviour of those elements in other and simpler circumstances. Our answer would be that if our thought-model of the elements is satisfactory, it is capable of suggesting, by the rules of implication, if these again are satisfactory, any event or combination which the elements themselves are capable of achieving, by causal interaction. That is to say, correct thinking should find no new whole or function to be inevitably beyond its grasp; if it fails, it is not that complete knowledge of the elements is insufficient, as asserted by emergent evolution, but that the knowledge of the elements was insufficient, and could have been remedied by further investigation of their properties in quite simple combinations, or even in no combinations at all.

Memory and the power to learn have also their analogies in mechanism. A piece of spring steel may bear signs of its previous history of strain (i.e. 'fatigue'); indeed, everything bears some mark of its past, and the difference between the 'memory' of a stone and of one of Hull's conditioned reflex models is only one of degree. The same applies to learning, which seems to be the modification of the response of an instrument by other factors, past or present, affecting it. Again, human memory and learning have a vivid, conscious aspect, and an astonishing elasticity and power of grasping principles which no machine has hitherto imitated and which may be in the power of conscious processes alone. But as no one has ever devised any 'test' for consciousness it is impossible to decide whether or not the most elaborate man-made machines also show this power. We only infer the presence of consciousness like our own in other human beings because their outward appearance and neural mechanisms are similar; and naturally this analogy can tell us nothing in the case of mechanisms or even lower animals which are admittedly very unlike us in many of the features which we can observe. But the apparent simplicity of thought and action, introspectively examined, and the apparent absence of clanking machinery should not lead us to disregard the actuality of mechanisms which physiology can show to be involved in these very processes.

Introspective psychology and analytical philosophy of the self, of perception and of will, do not seem to take into account that in any well-made machine one is ignorant of the working of most of the parts—the better they work, the less are we conscious of them. Thus it is very unlikely that introspection will reveal those intermediate processes which are most important. Physiological evidence as to levels (e.g. the integration of muscular movements in spinal reflexes) shows how much organisation is achieved at non-conscious levels. Again, it is only a fault which draws our attention to the existence of a mechanism at all; hence the value of evidence from neuropathology. We are particularly apt to pass over purposive activity as so natural that it requires no explanation (cf. phototropism, growth of terminal and axillary buds, and auxines in plants).

Greater mechanical complexity often leads to greater simplicity and co-ordination of performance. An aeroplane is more complicated than a pile of stones, but its performance is more unified. Those who assert that physiological theories of the action of the nervous system could explain only complexity and not such supposedly 'simple' things as consciousness, thought, colours, and images seem to forget that there are several ways of putting the parts of an engine together. You can drop them all into a bucket, in which case the complexity is fairly high but the simplicity of performance nil; or you can put them together correctly and let the engine start, in which case the complexity is in a sense greater because now there is relational as well as atomic complexity and the possibility of performance is increased, yet at the same time there has entered a new simplicity and co-ordination very like that of a living organism.

Once the dangers of introspection are recognised, many psychological questions become much less perplexing. We have no obligation to decide in a definite manner whether or not the utilisation of clues in perception is or is not interpretation. We can admit that these clues are utilised and can say that all perceptual and thinking processes are continuous with the workings of the external world and of the nervous system. There is then no hard and fast line between the unconscious, effortless use of clues and laborious conscious interpretation. Neither is there any hard and fast line between an action like walking over smooth ground which can become so automatic that it is accomplished by the lower nervous centres and the same act of walking with great care and attention on a narrow mountain ledge; it is a matter of different levels of neural activity. So also some processes, ordinarily considered to involve thought, can become so automatic that they leave higher levels vacant for simultaneous thought on other topics, and the question whether a man can think of two different things at the same time becomes entirely a matter of the definition of the processes involved. The more interesting problem is the nature of the mechanisms.

There is considerable evidence that it is illegitimate to separate thought completely from feeling. As pointed out previously many discoveries, even of the most intellectual nature, emerge into gradual clarity from a state of mind where a feeling of preference for one method over another is often the guiding principle. As an illustration, if we look at a faulty geometrical proof we may have a vague feeling of dissatisfaction with some portion which directs our attention to the fallacy, before we have consciously realised where it lies. Perhaps, then, when the concepts or 'stations' in thought are not sufficiently precise to emerge as conscious images they may show themselves as vague feelings, such as those which determine us in the choice of words in a sentence. Similar views have been expressed by MacCurdy. Perhaps frustrated nervous activity occasions pain and sorrow and successful activity pleasure, as in Aristotle's theory of pleasure and pain. This would account for this directive power of feeling upon thought, and for Thorndike's law of effect.

It is possible that such vague feelings play a large part in the advancing of new scientific hypotheses and in the production of works of art. The main difference is that the scientist should not regard his feelings as proof that his hypothesis is right; he must be thankful for whatever inarticulate thoughts and emotions have suggested a new hypothesis, but he must test it by experiment. The artist does not do this; he relies on the fullness of this inner feeling of satisfaction, and the acceptance or rejection of his work by other men, to establish the truth or falsity of his expression of reality; and the greater artist he is, the greater will be the field of thought and experience from which these inarticulate feelings and purposes arise, and the greater their chance of expressing ideas and facts that are fundamental in general experience. Perhaps, also, the means by which art produces its effects are akin to neural facilitation. An extra stimulus is known to elicit a reflex which the appropriate stimulus is too weak to effect. We must all have sometime felt, in reading or listening to music, that we very nearly had had the same thoughts or feelings of our own accord, but that the artist has elicited them where we failed, and that he has made articulate what was inarticulate before. Indeed, a wit has been defined as 'one who says the things we should have said if we had thought of them'. Perhaps most of us have also had the feeling of being, ourselves, in an unusually musical mood when we have come back from a concert, or have even naïvely started to write a novel in the fresh glow of having read one. Children imitating the tricks in a circus they have just seen, or adults repeating wireless slogans or newspaper headlines perhaps exemplify the same phenomenon of facilitation. Its main features would be that it assists the completion and expression of thoughts or feelings or associations of ideas which our own minds were too small or dissociated to achieve, and consequently gives some feeling of satisfaction and freedom from frustration of our thinking. At the same time, as in propaganda, it may lead to the facilitation of thinking along shaky lines at the expense of less articulate but sounder thought.

This theory of the continuity of man and his physical and human environment seems to illuminate some old ethical problems such as hedonism.

No doubt it is possible to show that all our acts are done because to leave them undone would cause us to be more unhappy—or at least because we imagine that it would be so; the unhappiness might result simply from our own immediate loss or pain, or future loss at the hands of others whom we have wronged, or from a kind of 'sympathy' which causes us to be pained at the sight of suffering in others and so leads us to avoid this purely selfish pain. But the hedonist seems to forget that this latter type of pain actually involves the appreciation of the feelings of others as such and that it is impossible in considering ordinary acts of so-called unselfishness to draw any division between ourselves and other people as would be necessary for his theory. No doubt the immediate spring of our act as introspectively observed may be a feeling that we should be less happy if we acted differently; but we should be unhappier because the scope of our brains or minds is such as to take into consideration the rights and desires of other people; otherwise what is there to give rise to the feeling of unhappiness? Thus our brains and minds are part of a continuous causal chain which includes the minds and brains of other men, and it is senseless to stop short in tracing the springs of our ordinary, co-operative acts. If our acts are far-sighted and well-adapted they are bound not to be entirely selfish; for our sense-organs and brains are capable of putting us in contact with the outer world of things and people and of realising their equivalence with ourselves. It is impossible to explain our feelings of willingness or reluctance to do certain acts except in terms of the feelings which they would arouse in other people; and that already demonstrates that the feelings of those people enter as a part of the things we consider in our conduct, and therefore that our actions are not purely hedonistic.

Again, extremely selfish and hedonistic activity is possible; some men are more prone to it than others. Probably such selfish and pleasure-seeking activity can usually be seen in its true colours by trying certain substitutions in the activity and seeing whether they affect the man's attitude. To take a very simple and crude example, if we wish to decide how far a scientist's interest in research is genuine, we can offer him an equal salary for turning out advertisements for a patent medicine, or running a business, or for continuing his research. It is often found that the selfish man or the hedonist accepts such substitutions easily, or even initiates them. He appears, perhaps, to be interested in his work above all things, but will abandon it for easier monetary gain; or he will do his best to break up some scientific establishment in whose progress he seemed absorbed, rather than resign its management to other, equally capable, hands. He chooses as his friend whosoever at that moment supports and flatters him, rather than a man whose opinion he has considered trustworthy in the past, but who differs from him.

It may be objected that the scientist who is 'really' absorbed in his work is only trying to win a wider and more lasting approval from humanity; he realises that monetary gain at the expense of commercialisation and insincerity are cheap compared with the approval of present and future men, as an earnest and 'disinterested' scientist. The difficulty which classical ethics has always found in giving definite disproof of such statements is, it seems to me, due to its committing the same fallacy as hedonism. It tries to assign the causation of any act to some definite spring or motive— hedonism to personal pleasure seeking; classical ethics to an idea of the good, a moral sentiment, or a sense of duty. But perhaps it is possible to show that any act is not due to any one of these causes because the causation of an act is of quite another type. An act is surely one stage in a continuous causal process—the process of interaction between man with his psychological and physiological mechanism and the mechanism of the world outside him, and other men. In other words, for the classical moralist, all is lost if he cannot prove, in argument with the hedonist, that the spring of an action is definitely an idea of the good and a wish to do it or something of that nature. He is forced to exclude the complexity of the actual intellectual and emotional content of action as much as the hedonist. On our view any man is part of a causally connected universe, and his actions are part of the continuous interaction taking place in it. Consequently it is absurd to make *a priori* generalisations as to the springs of action; we must look at particular cases and find how wide a region of this causal chain they involve; we must ask whether they involve merely the satisfaction of an appetite for food or an appetite involving half the man's intellectual equipment or knowledge; whether they involve merely the refusal to be crossed or contradicted, or the wider refusal to entertain any notion if the most persevering effort can find objections to it. What we want then is not a hypothetical common causative factor in all acts—a feeling, an idea or a drive—which can be discovered to be self-centred or altruistic, to involve expert knowledge or not to involve it. We want to find what processes and knowledge any particular act involves; what width of contact with other men's discoveries and desires it contains. This may not always be easily discoverable; conscious or unconscious hypocrisy is common. But in the end one should be able to say what is involved in a particular act—what range of sympathy and consideration and intellectual knowledge and foresight; and this will determine the degree to which the act might be called selfish or hedonistic. But the essential point is that we are not seeking a primary cause—a spring of action—because we do not think that such exists; we ask, instead, how large a part of reality—of the external world and of other men's thoughts and wishes—is influential in any given act of a particular man.

If we consider adaptation to environment as one of the most fundamental principles of behaviour, it is possible to find some explanation for hysterical conduct. This seems to consist in adapting oneself by excluding all parts of the environment to which one's powers and attitudes are inadequate; a form of adaptation is thus achieved by narrowing and distorting the environment until one's conduct appears adequate to it, rather than by altering one's conduct and enlarging one's knowledge till one can cope with the larger, real environment. Dissociation and schizophrenia and repression are further mechanisms for attaining this state of splendid isolation and pseudo-adjustment and of excluding difficulties and awkward suspicions. T. H. Huxley called it 'the hypostasis of men's hopes', and it has been familiarised by the psycho-analysts as 'wishful thinking'. Hence arise the hysterical symptoms in the asseveration of these 'truths'— the emphasis on their sanctity and immunity from criticism or argument; the refusal to admit their analogy with other human phenomena such as pre-scientific opinion on scientific problems, when this has since proved to be wrong; the strengthening of belief by formula, repetition, ritual and pseudo-scientific system. The result, as seen by an unsympathetic observer, is a series of repetitive actions and justifications for them, closely analogous to the exaggerated and neurotic conduct of a man who washes his hands a hundred times a day, or hesitates a hundred times before crossing the road, or requires to have his self-confidence reassured every moment of the day by fresh praise and new successes. A religious belief may have objective truth behind it; but at least we can say that few if any religious men realise that their own assertion of their convictions is closely paralleled by neurotic behaviour where it has been clearly proved that ritual and asseveration are no proof of objective truth or of real motive.

If this theory happens to be true it would help to bring hysterical behaviour within the scope of a general theory of activity and of pleasure and pain. On this theory conduct, and its affective tone, would be largely determined by the success or frustration of the organism's impulses and wishes, when it is in contact with reality, as delimited by the scope of its sense-organs and co-ordinating powers and by the presence or absence of tendencies to dissociation and repression.

Why much neurotic behaviour should take such peculiar forms as it does, is a mystery. Why should the units of a neurosis appear, from psycho-analysis, to be fantasies, legends and actions, rather than physiological blockages? But the difficulty does not seem to be insuperable; on any theory of behaviour we must contemplate the integration of physiological units into higher behavioural ones and even, perhaps, into more general concepts and archetypes of thought.

A number of problems, such as error, paradox, and illusion, can be approached on this theory, for we seek to give a genetic or aetiological explanation of their origin in the functioning of the neural mechanism, rather than an ontological explanation of them as if they were ultimate and unanalysable things.

The two principal kinds of error—errors of perception or illusions, and errors of thought, would be attributed to the 'misinterpretation' or confusion of different stimuli or patterns of excitation in the brain. This is not unknown in mechanisms which show some power of perception or recognition. For example, an instrument for separating green from red apples by means of a photocell with colour filters would be 'tricked' or 'deceived' into grouping a red block of wood or ball of paper with the red apples.

Confusion of two similar concepts is a fruitful cause of erroneous thinking. (I am particularly addicted to it, and if ever I conceive any original idea, it will be because I have been abnormally prone to confuse ideas, but have just saved myself by experimental verification, and have thus found remote analogies and relations which others have not considered! Others rarely make these confusions, and proceed by precise analysis.) Another cause of error, analogous in many ways, is the inclusion in the statement of a problem of vague and indefinite concepts, infinite series, and so on. Thus the problem of the distance travelled by the fly between two converging trains or of the man whose train arrived an hour early are almost insoluble if treated in terms of the distances which form infinite convergent series but easily soluble in terms of the times which are definite and fixed. (The vagueness of other concepts such as 'government', 'wealth', 'rights' and so forth is a source of error in political thinking and prediction, but is so hard to exemplify by instances that are not themselves open to differences of opinion that we may neglect them for the present.) Ambiguous or infinite concepts are perhaps, to the mind, what a continual movement of the figure-setting keys on a calculating machine would be; they prevent the problem from ever being set unambiguously to the machine. Further similar confusions of concepts may occur at later stages in the reasoning, and are like a response of a pawl to a wrong tooth because it juts nearly high enough—a factor which caused some difficulty in early calculating machines.

So far we have been discussing mainly problems which have been set in a confusing form. We have also to decide why it is that the clearest minds extract the definite and workable concepts from the problem, and so set it to themselves in a soluble manner. Apart from emotional factors, such as dogmatic attitudes to certain problems, the main influence is probably habit and practice, in hinting when a vague concept has been chosen and suggesting the promising type of concept to look for. Here again, there is some hope for the extremely muddle-headed, since perseverance will always show where the choice of concept and method has been bad, by resulting in failure to solve the problem. If we honestly admit our failure and do not have recourse to dogma and belief we may sooner or later hit upon a more promising method of approach.

In the same way we can give an aetiological explanation of paradoxes such as the case of the Cretan who said that all Cretans were liars, or the proposition, 'All universal propositions are false.' It is very difficult to give a satisfactory explanation of the ontological status, reference, and logical classification of such paradoxes if we once admit that all propositions carry as it were the right to apply to something objectively real. But if we regard them simply as expressions of the working of a kind of telephone exchange then it is easy to see that some may express external reality correctly while others may be meaningless, self-contradictory, or extremely tangled. For instance, if one had a switch which put all the extensions in one office on to the public telephone line—a kind of class-membership situation in which the public line represents the class of all the extensions—and if one accidentally wired up this public line as if it were one of the extensions, one would get some peculiar 'speak-back' effects in the lines which would rather resemble the confused circularity of our thinking when we try to clear up one of these paradoxes on verbal and logical lines.

The same applies to the limitations of thought in dealing with external reality. For instance, it may be said that this theory is proved to be wasted effort, and to contain a fallacy by the fact that the mechanisms it *does* postulate do *not* work in the last extreme; it postulates classical mechanics, Euclidean space, and logical rules which do not fit the evasive behaviour of space, time and electrons.

The answer seems to me to be this: we have not been claiming that human thought is sublimely free to pursue obscure phenomena through their strange spaces and times; on the contrary, we have argued that thought is a term for the conscious working of a highly complex machine, built of parts having dimensions where the classical laws of mechanics are still very nearly true, and having dimensions where space is, to all intents and purposes, Euclidean. This mechanism, I have argued, has the power to represent, or parallel, certain phenomena in the external world as a calculating machine can parallel the development of strains in a bridge. It follows that this machine will parallel—and so be able to 'give an account of' or 'predict' most easily—those phenomena whose mechanism most resembles itself—that is, processes where the classical laws of mechanics are true. If it fails, in the end, to represent in itself microscopic phenomena obeying different laws this will merely mean that the mind—itself an instrument like a microscope—is faced with a situation to which it is inapplicable, as a microscope is inapplicable to the resolution of points nearer than half the wave-length of the light employed. This will mean that the structure of the brain, as well as the structure of all measuring instruments, sets a limit to causal explanation of the very small—the one because it is ill-suited to representing their strange processes, the other because measurement disturbs the thing being measured. But it will not mean that interdependence is unreal, and that causal explanations are a misinterpretation of statistical results; the interdependence of things will remain, as before, proved by the macroscopic effects. I do not mean to suggest that this limit of thought has already been reached; the powers of one mechanism to imitate another are remarkable, and by suitable conventions the most evasive and paradoxical phenomena may be represented in terms of a rigid mechanism. But even if such thought *does* finally fail to describe the facts consistently I do not see that it will mean that its causal interpretation of the nature of the world, based on its representation of the larger objects in that world which it is more fitted to represent, is wrong.

Again, it may be objected that we have failed to account for the absolute precision with regard to quantities obtainable in mathematical and geometrical proof. Geometrical proof is, in essentials, the application to space of the reasoning $A = B$, $B = C$, therefore $A = C$. But whence, it may be asked, comes its absolute precision? It is to be noted that its precision is of a peculiar kind, gained at the expense of versatility and width of application. A ruler, for instance, may be less precise than Pythagoras's theorem in the result which it gives for the length of the third side of a right-angled triangle; but it can tell us, to a certain degree of precision, the lengths of the sides of innumerable other triangles of which Pythagoras's theorem can tell us nothing. Error is due, in measurement, to the confusion of two magnitudes which are not quite equal; our measuring instruments cause us to judge two magnitudes equal when they differ slightly. We can reduce the extent of this error indefinitely by increasing the accuracy of the measuring instruments, but can never quite avoid it. In geometry, on the other hand, we obtain perfect accuracy in a limited field by narrowing our attention to magnitudes so dissimilar that they cannot be confused; all magnitudes in geometry are defined as equal or unequal; we are not concerned with the very nearly equal. It is comparable to the precision, at the expense of flexibility, obtained in law where, for instance, the conscription age is fixed by a certain precise date of birth, rather than by physique, etc.

With regard to the place of pleasure and pain and ideals and moral aims in this theory, the assumption best in accord with fact would seem to be that pleasure accompanies successful activity, and pain frustration, much as in Aristotle's theory as mentioned above. This, of course, can lead to endless complexity, as temporary frustration can be the means to greater success in the end; and the frustration of one's own immediate pleasure can be sought in order to obtain the happiness of another. For, as we pointed out in discussing hedonism, if we are part of the world of men and things, and if our brains are capable of modelling greater or smaller parts of reality, we should find just such subordination of immediate pleasure to wider aims. Still the doctrine would be fundamentally relativistic or 'subjectivistic', in that people's moral ideals will only coincide in so far as those of their mental and emotional and physiological processes which are concerned are similar; if they differ in opinions, we must not just condemn them for failing to see and appreciate an objective good. If they were mules or birds, their objective goods would be different; and the most we can say, on the objective side, is that certain conduct is more generally satisfactory, and socially more useful, than others. The emotional and intellectual satisfaction and idea of right and good which accompanies this would remain a subjective thing, conditioned by the degree of frustration or success occurring in the psycho-neural activity of the particular person to whom we are talking.

Our theory has some bleaker consequences. What becomes of purposes and ideals and creative art and thought? What is knowledge, if we are but a part of the mechanical system of the world we seek to know? What becomes of our ceaseless effort to explain the universe we live in, if explanation is but a part of the mechanical process? If conflicts are the result of clashing neural patterns, what hope is there of overcoming them? If happiness is the result of the success of our own neural processes, linked with the world yet finally limited by the mechanical complexity of our particular brains, what reason is there to set one ideal above another when two men are found to be in conflict? A great deal of the argument against materialism has always consisted in drawing attention to the highest achievements of the

human mind and soul and free will and pointing out the
contrast between this and the drab, stereotyped working of
a machine, as if the idea of a connection between the two
would at once appear too ridiculous for further thought.
It has been customary, from the days of T. H. Huxley to
those of L. Hogben, to point to these materialists, as they
lecture, and say that they, speaking, thinking, seeking after
truth, are living disproof of their own theories. Clearly, if
a materialist denies that he is conscious, or has thoughts that
sometimes do not issue in action, or if he represents himself
as a machine which is too simple to accomplish what he
accomplishes, he deserves criticism; but few have done this.
It is really the scornful audience who deserve criticism for
blindly refusing to consider whether things are always what
they seem—whether their own powers of introspection are
able to tell them the secrets of their own mental processes
and whether many of their own acts are not very similar
to those of the machines, natural and man-made, which lie
all round them and which they will not take the trouble
to understand. I am not criticising them for refusing to
accept the theory, but for refusing to consider it and to do
experiments which might settle some of these problems one
way or the other. This is the one form of intolerance I
heartily approve—an intolerance for those who will not try
experiments but prefer to be dogmatic, whether dogmatic
materialists or dogmatic vitalists. Those who dislike experiment profess to be shocked at the idea of tampering with
such great and sacred issues; it is 'to botanise upon your
mother's grave'. But they themselves rely on experiment
in many matters—in every case where they find a successful
mode of living and behaving under novel circumstances.
What objection have they to experiment in these other
fields? I can see none except laziness, wishful thinking and
the 'desire to be right', or else a culpable failure to distin-

guish between the true and false experimenter. Undoubtedly there are some very hard-headed and unsympathetic scientists, political reformers, and innovators of all kinds who disguise as experiment a dogmatic scorn and rejection of everything which their parents and the previous generation had accepted, whether by experiment or tradition. But this is not true *experiment*.

If our theory were established by experiment—a very remote possibility—it would imply, among other things, that consciousness, as we know it, depends on the particular organisation of our own nervous systems and is inseparable from them; the soul would not be immortal. But as regards our knowledge and purposes within this world I do not see that we should have destroyed anything. To those in sympathy with this attitude, there is something wonderful in the idea that man's brain is the greatest machine of all, imitating within its tiny network events happening in the most distant stars, predicting their appearances with accuracy, and finding in this power of successful prediction and communication the ultimate feature of consciousness. Further, I see no great difficulty in understanding how anything so 'different' from physical objects and concepts and reasoning can tell us something more about those physical objects; for I see no reason to suppose that the processes of reasoning *are* fundamentally different from the mechanism of physical nature. On our model theory neural or other mechanisms can imitate or parallel the behaviour and interaction of physical objects and so supply us with information on physical processes which are not directly observable to us. Our thought, then, has objective validity because it is not fundamentally different from objective reality but is specially suited for imitating it—that is our suggested answer. It sets no crabbed limit to the attempt of thought to understand and express the universe.

CHAPTER VII

Methods of testing this hypothesis. Discussion of possible criticisms. Summary

JUST as in physics, so in psychology, physiology and philosophy it is necessary to do experiments in order to find clearly what are the facts that need explanation, and then more experiments to test out hypothetical explanations that have been advanced.

There seems to me to have been too great a disregard for experiment in finding the different 'meanings' of words, concepts, ideas, purposes, and other problems of philosophy. We may attempt an inductive investigation of the meaning of two important words—'meaning' and 'proof'—as illustrations. We are not claiming that the meaning of a word is to be found by combining *all* possible usages; for some usages are confused or stupid or inconsistent with each other, just as some instances of the operation of gravitation are confused and masked by frictional interference; we want to find numbers of 'good' instances (judged by their consistency and repeatability) just as we endeavour to find good experimental situations and methods in physics. As mentioned in the Introduction, Plato in the first book of the *Republic* and many other philosophers have analysed the meaning of words, but usually they have been anxious to obtain an exact definition or to be able to point to a perfect Idea at any cost; the conception of a somewhat indefinite, yet fruitful, meaning to be found by patient analysis of a number of usages, seems often to have escaped them.

A word, with its everyday usage, is a thing to be regarded with great respect, for it is a tool which has usually been found to fit some aspect of a complicated reality sufficiently well to enable practical results to be obtained. As in all induction, a great deal of the rough selection of likely common features must be done rather on the basis of feelings of similarity and dissimilarity than on more explicit grounds. Since the meaning of 'meaning' is of importance in the present enquiry (being closely connected with the problems of symbolism and implication) we may attempt such an analysis of it.

Examples of the word 'meaning'

'I don't know what you mean' =
> 'I don't know what thing or relation you are referring to' or 'I do not understand your language' or 'Your language is so complicated that it does not signify any proposition, does not constitute a proof that lets me rest satisfied, frustrates my thinking', etc.

'I mean to do so-and-so' =
> 'I intend to' = (on determinist theories) 'I am being determined to make plans for doing so-and-so.'

'I mean what I say' =
> 'I am serious; my words can be taken at their literal meaning' (in the true sense of meaning discussed below).

'Mensa means table' =
> 'Mensa is the Latin equivalent for table in English.'

'A red sky in the morning means rain' or 'That noise means that a joint has blown' =
> 'is empirically or causally connected with'.

'Chair means an article of furniture for sitting on' =
> 'The word chair symbolises an article of furniture for sitting on.'

In general, we may distinguish first of all between *meaning* and *particular meaning*, or the possession of meaning. Thus in the first sense we say 'His meaning was clear', which is not the same as saying 'He meant the word "clear"'. Calling these respectively *meaning* and *a meaning* (since these appear to be the customary terms), we can examine the above sentences. Some of the senses seem only indirectly connected with each other, and are almost slang usages; e.g. meaning as equivalent to purpose or seriousness or causal connection in the outer world or an object referred to. All these senses would be interesting to investigate, but the usages peculiar to the word 'meaning' are more important, e.g. '"Chair" means an article of furniture for sitting on', where the meaning is not the physical article referred to, but something more like the definition or concept itself; or again, 'Your meaning is not clear'. The algebraic symbol x has *meaning* but not *a meaning* until it has had *a meaning* assigned to it in a particular mathematical argument. The common feature of all these usages is perhaps that 'meaning' or meaningfulness is the power of symbols to refer to objects or things; while 'a meaning' is the total symbolic equivalent of the thing—i.e. all the associated ideas, the connotation, the universal concept, etc., and in less rigid parlance sometimes the actual object *referred* to. When we think of any object, its uniqueness and nature determine to a great extent whether we think mainly of it or of its properties; in the latter case 'meaning' and in the former case 'reference' plays the greater part in our thought. Thus, we talk of the meaning of the word 'chair', 'granite', or even 'phœnix', for in all cases we are thinking mainly of the kind of properties possessed by the thing, even where it is the only member of its class (real or imaginary); but where we are concerned with a single object (e.g. Westminster Abbey or the English Channel) it is more appropriate to talk of 'reference' than of 'meaning'. The same applies to proper names of people, whether there be only one or many having that name. Thus *a meaning* seems most applicable to the total symbolic equivalent (i.e. all the associated ideas and synonyms) of an object, where the object, either by its commonness, or by the superior interest of its properties over its identity, is not presented to the mind very strongly. Where, on the other hand, we think of one object or person (e.g. Westminster Abbey or a friend of ours) known to us by acquaintance or reputation, the self-identity of the object or person takes precedence over the sum total of its symbolic equivalents and associated ideas, and it is more appropriate to talk of 'reference' than of 'meaning'.

It would be interesting to analyse those subtle shades of feeling which lead us to judge such and such a use of a word correct or incorrect, and to feel satisfied with one synonym or analysis of it and not with another. Probably anyone who reads this will feel that I have made exactly the wrong analysis and approved the wrong usages! The existence of such inarticulate guidance from feelings is another argument for the view that popular usage of words is not merely loose and inaccurate, but indicates something very profound about the way in which we are led to use certain words to describe particular situations.

MEANINGLESSNESS

There appear to be three main types of meaninglessness:

(1) The use of a term to which no meaning has ever been assigned; e.g. the word 'dink'.

(2) The combination, to form a compound noun or verb, phrase or sentence of two logically inconsistent terms; e.g. 'square circle' or 'The top is the bottom'.

(3) The combination, to form a compound noun or verb, phrase or sentence of two terms describing events or objects which do not, in our experience, occur in that combination (e.g. 'The blackboard on that wall', pointing to a wall on which there is no blackboard, or 'inflammable water'). We

have to be much more careful with this usage than with the others, since on the one hand it merges from meaninglessness into falsity (e.g. 'Water encourages a match to burn'), and on the other hand, into what may be correct, either literally or metaphorically. Thus later scientific knowledge may prove the truth of statements that at one time seemed absurd and meaningless (e.g. the mass of light), and there may be a literary veracity in describing a landscape as patient or a wind as angry.

What is the relevance of all this to our theory of thought and implication? Mainly this, perhaps: when an object is perceived, or thought of in terms of symbols, various associative events may occur; we may think of some relevant property of that object, or of some other object, or we may think of, or even have a visual image of, some particular object. All these are closely connected with the mechanism by which symbols can retain fixed reference and be combined in such a way as to represent future events and make prediction possible; this power of symbols to represent and forecast events—or in mechanical terms, the nature of the mechanism which enables them to do it—is just what we have been suggesting as the meaning of 'meaning'.

Again, let us consider the word 'proof'.

Proof may be formally defined as any method of demonstrating the truth of a proposition, though this does not really help.

Usages. Proof of Pythagoras's theorem = Deductive argument.

'These tracks prove that the car passed here' = the tracks show that the car passed—they indicate an objective fact rather than something about a proposition.

'The occurrence of this bacillus in all these cases of cholera, together with its absence in normal persons, proves beyond reasonable doubt that it is the cause of cholera' = Inductive proof.

'Proofs' of the existence of God (e.g. cosmological and ontological); in our view, speculative completions, on insufficient data, of the incomplete reality we experience, in accordance mainly with wishes and ideals. Other philosophical proofs:

(1) Critical (showing inconsistencies in common-sense statements).

(2) Sceptical—asserting such inconsistencies to be insuperable and to invalidate all positive statements (scepticism should at least be sceptical as to its own justification in making such a positive assertion).

(There are other senses, only indirectly connected, such as printer's proofs, the 'Proof plane' of Victorian physicists, which = 'testing plane' and the words 'waterproofing' or 'fireproofing', derived presumably from their ability to render substances unassailable by water or fire, as a proof renders a proposition unassailable by criticism. The common factor is 'goodness', as in the Latin *probus*.)

Induction has already been discussed. Our argument is that it is almost infinitely improbable that we should experience the regular sequences which we do experience unless possible appearances are continually restricted by preceding ones, and that these restrictions bear investigation only in terms of space and of persistent objects. The second part of induction—the particular methods of observing agreement, difference, and concomitant variation over long periods—are necessitated by the fairly high probability of certain 'chance' or 'misleading' (i.e. causally indirect) conjunctions in this realm of already restricted possibilities. If the associative mechanism of our minds is to contain a true rather than a false copy of reality it must therefore have some kind of 'delay action' which causes it to acquire strong patterns only from repeated experience (or from impressions so related to other conjunctions as to give them equal precedence).

Philosophical proof of the critical type has also been roughly investigated. It seems to consist in showing inconsistencies between ordinary statements, generally by showing contradictions among the 'implications' and associations of those concepts. Thus, objects are ordinarily held to exist in space, and their colours to exist likewise; but coloured illumination, darkness, or colour-blindness in the observer changes the 'colour' of objects and yet seems to make no difference to the objects or to the space, so that the colours do not seem to exist in space quite in the same way that the objects do. Since every concept (it has been argued) is a very ambiguous and precarious symbol of a part of reality it is not surprising that such confusions arise. They give ground, it seems to me, for a general investigation of the nature of knowledge by experimental methods rather than for logical tricks played with concepts as if they were hard, precise counters in a game.

Two other types of proof remain:

Causal proof in terms of *familiar causal conjunctions*, as, for example, the track of tyres 'proves' that a car has passed. This type of proof employs the type of 'synthetic' implication and inference which we have described as artificial causation in which symbols are substituted for objects and rules for causal interaction. On our 'model' theory the symbols become states or patterns in the nervous system and the rules the mode of interconnection and consequently of mutual excitation between these patterns. Owing to its synthetic nature and its connection with the logically disreputable regions of the causal and the empirical this type of proof (probably the commonest in ordinary thinking) has perhaps received insufficient consideration from philosophers in general.

The last type of proof is *Deductive*, including syllogistic, geometrical, and algebraic.

An essential type of such reasoning employs the axiom that two things which are equal to the same thing are equal to one another. In geometry it may often consist of a longer train such as (representing angles, lengths, etc., as *a*, *b*, or *c*) $a=b$; but $b=c$, and $c=d$; therefore $a=d$, Q.E.D. The train of argument serves merely to bring within one's grasp a series of associations whose length or complication prevents the first step and the last from being grasped simultaneously by the ordinary person. It is well known that the number of steps in a mathematical or geometrical argument can be reduced or increased considerably at will.

But two important problems now arise: First, how is it possible for such reasoning to give, as it undoubtedly does, perfect precision in regard not only to empty symbols such as letters but in regard to ideal constructions in space, such as circles and triangles? And secondly, does this perfect precision in regard, not to empirical objects but to ideal objects, indicate some transcendent power of thought, inimitable by mechanical models, and grasping eternal realities as was supposed by the Platonics?

As we have already suggested, the apparent precision of geometrical reasoning in dealing with external objects such as triangles does not indicate transcendence of the empirical; it only means that the extreme and most clear-cut instances are chosen in the external world and are symbolised by concepts so few in number and so different from one another that no inexactness, and very little confusion of thought, is possible in reasoning with them. The exactness, in other words, is gained at the expense of the ability to deal with all the gradations of quantities found in the external world. In just the same way we might work out a logical system about the inheritance of red or black hair, which might apply rigidly for the extreme cases but could not be applied to the great majority of people whose hair is intermediate in shade.

On our theory, the reason why we tend so continually to 'classify' reality into objects is that adaptation and life are otherwise impossible, just as it is difficult to use an electric light without a switch in the circuit, though this is an artificial point at which the flow of current is interrupted. In general, the constitution of our senses—for instance, their restricted ranges of response—exaggerate the differences between objects into rigid boundaries. Radiant heat for instance seems to be quite a different sort of 'thing' from light, just because it is received by different sense-organs; and this sensory difference tends to be regarded as a feature of the world external to our sense-organs.

THE PLACE OF EXTERNAL MODELS AND ANALOGIES IN EXPLANATION

It is clear that a model can be very misleading; I do not feel that Mrs Ladd Franklin's analogy (in Helmholtz, *Phys. Optics*, Eng. trans. vol. II, p. 467) of the chemical combinations of a particular aniline dye strengthens her colour theory; and an over-simplified model may prevent one investigating slight anomalies of the real process which conceal further interesting mechanisms, and perhaps mechanisms that are exceptionally under our control. Thus both academic and practical gain may be sacrificed.

Perhaps the most culpable use of physical models in scientific research is where the analogy of one among many possible mechanisms is taken to prove that the actual mechanism at work in some phenomenon is exactly, or closely, similar. On the other hand, if we can show by argument and experiment that, within our experience, there is only one type of mechanism which can perform as we see the problematical mechanism performing (e.g. give rise to certain visible results, though the mechanism itself is too small and delicate to investigate directly), then there is some presumption in favour of that mechanism being actually at work, just because the chances against its occurrence are not so very great, being zero in our sample of experience; this evidence may be further strengthened by other evidence as to the identity of the physical elements or compounds likely to be involved. Thus, models of bio-electric potentials involving only electrolytes and membranes are more likely to indicate the actual processes than those involving metal electrodes and insulated wires.

The most satisfactory function of models and analogies seems to be a more general one—to indicate the *kind* of mechanism necessary to produce the results found. Thus a model may show that earthquakes and geological faults are due to certain types of stress; or a mechanical or electrical model may show that the correct response of a barograph to changes of pressure independently of changes in temperature must involve some thermal-correction device. The greater the number of possible models, all of which would serve to illustrate the same general point, the safer is the use of models and analogies, for this purpose; for we are now concerned not with a high probability that the *actual* mechanism is the same in the model and the reality, but with the probability that the *type* of mechanism is the same; and the fewer the general types of mechanism that we can conceive, the better the analogy, no matter how many exact methods of illustrating it may be found. (I mean by a type of mechanism such a thing as the *principle of correction*, and as particular ways of illustrating it, a thermally corrected barometer, automatic volume control in wireless receivers, etc.)

But, it may be asked, why employ such models at all? Why not use linguistic, diagrammatic, or, best of all, mathematical representations of the real processes? I think there are various reasons, which may apply in different cases. For instance, some people think more easily and fruitfully in terms of mechanism and things that can be visualised. But more important than this, a model gives a general indication of the kind of thing that can be mechanically achieved; and it seems to me that many persons are emotionally prejudiced against admitting how much mechanism can do, in the way of giving a flexible, well-adapted, subtle response to its surroundings. Adaptation, correction of one stimulus value by reference to others past and present, learning, modifiability, apparent simplicity of response on the part of a highly complicated machine, identification of common features in a complicated situation, overcoming of obstacles— all these things a machine can do; yet only the sight of an actual machine doing them will bring this home vividly to a number of people. It happens so often that even accomplished mathematicians and physicists lay down precise rules as to the limits of machines, the function of will, purpose, consciousness, and in general the difference between the man, who chooses what he will do, and the machine, which is part of a causal system. It seems to me most necessary therefore to show just how many of these essential processes involved in life and adaptation and survival and purpose are explicable from the causal end. We realise, surely, on the psychological level that there may be two aspects to a thing, and that the causally important aspect may not be the first to show up; may not a man say he feels he ought to retire from business when in reality he is being ousted from his position by outside persons and circumstances? Why then do we not consider the possibility that we often regard reality, in this way, back to front, and consider ourselves to be final sources of action when we are not, and to be introducing action of a totally different kind from anything physical when we are not? Spinoza made the same point, perhaps too forcibly, when he likened men to stones rolling down hill, asseverating all the while that they were choosing to roll down; for after all our brains are more elaborate, and capable of more, than the stone; but without this unnecessarily Swiftian touch the idea is surely worth investigating experimentally by whatever means serve best in a difficult and delicate realm both to indicate the real processes and to rid us of prejudices.

LLOYD MORGAN'S CANON, OCCAM'S RAZOR, AND SIMPLICITY IN EXPLANATION

It has often seemed difficult to account for the 'superiority' of a simple over a complicated explanation, both in regard to its emotional satisfactoriness and its correctness as tested by further experiment. The classical instance is the Copernican theory of the solar system as compared with Ptolemy's epicycle theory. The problem is complicated by the fact that a 'simple' explanation in this connection means one with a minimum of *ad hoc* postulates, rather than the one involving the simplest mechanical train of causation. Also we are not usually obliged to decide finally in favour of an explanation on the score of its simplicity alone; wrong theories indicate their failings by their inability to fit all the facts. Often the most satisfactory explanation is not the simplest suggested; it is only a general rule that the explanation involving the fewer new postulates is the more likely to be true, where it does seem to fit the facts as well as a theory involving more postulates.

Perhaps the reason is that the fewer the new postulates in the theory, the more probable is the existence of a phenomenon corresponding to that theory; for a phenomenon is the outcome of an assemblage of causes; and we might apply probability to such an assemblage of causes. Knowing the probability of each cause alone, the more causes we expect to find together in any chance assemblage, the more rarely will our expectation be fulfilled, just as we are very unlikely to find representatives of all the species of British birds, or of all the physical elements, in one place, i.e. in a given square mile. Now the number of causes which can be concerned in any given phenomenon is, in general, governed by their spatial proximity; and the fewer causes we expect to be gathered in any given extent of space, the more often will our expectation be fulfilled, i.e. the oftener will that phenomenon occur. (Of course this argument from probability does not conflict with causality; for this very distribution of causes is supposed to be determined by the interaction of so many causes that the particular effect of each is masked in the result; yet the action of those very causes is the one thing which accounts for the distribution in the result being what it is. In the same way, in firing at a target each of the causes—the amount of powder, the speed of its detonation, the effect of wind, the tension of the muscles in the arm that holds the rifle—are all subject to variations which have effects on the position of the bullet-hole on the target. The distribution of the bullet-holes is according to a certain law of chance, though all the determining causes were quite precise, because their combinations are so many. But it is only the underlying rigidity of the causal determination which produces *this* chance distribution.)

Thus the reason why the explanation involving the fewest new and independent postulates is most likely to be true is perhaps that a phenomenon corresponding to such an explanation is more likely than a phenomenon corresponding to an explanation involving more new postulates. In other words, the chance of a given explanation being correct is the product of the chances of a given train of (intermediate) events occurring, and of a certain explanation of it (the correct one) being advanced; and the more probable the train of events described by the explanation, the more likely is the real phenomenon to be of this nature, and the more probable therefore the correctness of that explanation.

One of the logical bases for using hypotheses and trying them out would seem to be as follows: If we have any set of objects causally related in certain ways they will occasion certain events; and the number of relations between n objects or events is $R = n(n-1) - 2n$, if we count relations 'A is related to B' and 'B is related to A' as separate, since a highly ingenious invention may often consist in no more than the reversal of a familiar relation. Similarly, a hypothesis about the objects A, B, etc., will give rise to as many hypothetical relations R, many of which may be open to experimental verification. Thus a small group of known facts gives rise to an enormous number of hypothetical and actual combinations, by whose agreement with each other the first observations of the facts and the hypothesis may be checked. Thus relations breed relations, as it were, and the further consistency of the system and its agreement with experiment gives a magnified view of the truth or falsity of the theory.

Other methods of testing the theory include electrophysiological studies of nerve impulses, anatomy, biochemistry, and model making. In regard to the latter, once we understand the properties of single nerve fibres and synapses fairly well it is possible that much will be learned from making simple, large-scale models of combinations of them, and recording the results produced, rather than from study of the actual spinal and cortical systems where everything is so small and delicate that it may never be practicable to trace the pattern of excitation involved in a complicated act.

Finally, we would emphasise again the importance of seeking the mechanism behind any simple, observable phenomenon such as a conditioned reflex rather than trying to explain more complicated facts in terms of this phenomenon. The modifiable mechanism which will account for the transfer of the salivary response from the tasting of meat to the sound of a bell may account also for much more—the modification of intelligent responses which never were reflexes. On the other hand, the mere modification of reflexes, as a phenomenon, will not account for responses, and modifications of responses, which never were reflexes at all. Thus, if I learn to play the piano, this is a modification of finger movements which I was always capable of but did not make spontaneously as reflexes. The emphasis is on the modifiable mechanism which sometimes shows itself in the modification of a reflex—not on the phenomenon of reflex modification. The conditioned reflex is thus an excellent experimental situation for studying modification of response and the mechanisms involved in it; it is not itself, as a phenomenon, the kind of unit from which a theory of thinking and action should be built. In the same way Koffka and the Gestalt psychologists seem to me to overstress the phenomenon of apparent psychological 'forces', at the expense of the mechanisms involved. The interesting thing in perception, surely, is not just *what* happens, but how and why it happens, and what has failed in the case of illusion or insanity. To go no further than the 'forces' is like explaining a railway collision by saying that the two trains were drawn together by a force. It is more fruitful to investigate the mechanism. Then, perhaps, we shall find that a brake failed or a signal jammed.

NEURAL ASSOCIATIONS IN THE BRAIN

On the figures given for the number of neurones in the human brain—approximately 10,000,000,000—and estimating the number of fibres in the sensory and motor nerves—both spinal and cerebral—as 3,000,000 and using the formula $n(n-1)/2 - n$ for the number of possible uni-directional connections between any number of objects, the total number of neurones in the brain should be some fifty times greater than it is, if every sensory and motor nerve were to be connected with every other. Interconnection of sensory with sensory and of motor with motor nerve fibres is postulated to allow of co-ordination of sensory experience, of reflexes, and so forth. It seems to be justified to some extent by what is known of the ganglion layers of the retina.

Models of the brain—on the pattern of a telephone exchange—would be much more convincing if they did not postulate any particular connections. Such constancy of connections is very unlikely in view of individual variations in micro-anatomy.

It is possible that a brain consisting of randomly connected impressionable synapses would assume the required degree of orderliness as a result of experience, just as a randomly connected telephone exchange might become usable if any pair of people could lower the resistance of their line and so get into audible communication, if they tried often enough.

The evidence for such a theory must depend largely on showing how far different parts of the brain can take over each other's functions. Lashley's work on relearning after experimental lesions tends to support this, as does evidence of relearning in human beings who have been aphasic or apraxic as a result of gun-shot wounds, as well as relearning motor performance after muscle transplantation. Experiments such as Stratten's with inverted spectacles, or other experiments with distorting spectacles which cause straight lines to appear curved, and learning of motor performances such as mirror drawing as well as the 'unrecognisability' of visual forms to patients who have gained their sight late in life, support the same view. Another source of evidence is clearly the study of children in whom specificity has not yet developed, but their immature powers of introspection and expression cause great difficulty. The best method would appear to be the artificial disturbance of co-ordinations, with a view to seeing which are the most plastic. The fundamental principle would seem to be that the co-ordinations which we utilise are those which fit in with reality—whether they be acquired or innate co-ordinations. If auditory, visual or tactual localisation, appreciation of posture, referred position of pain, touch, etc., can artificially be made to render experiences inconsistent with other sensory data, modification of our 'interpretation' of these sensations may take place in the course of time, till they once more become consistent with other sensations. Those which cannot be so altered are either very firmly impressed by experience or innate. But those which *can* be modified by artificial methods are surely not entirely innate, and if they are easily and completely altered, the chances of their having even an innate pre-set or tendency are very small.

It would be interesting to devise optical methods whereby the deliverances of touch and sight may be made inconsistent, but consistent if the sensations are otherwise 'interpreted' or differently localised or referred. Thus, one finger could be repeatedly touched by a pointer while it was made to appear, by a system of mirrors, as if a different finger was being touched. Such reassociation would presumably be slowest for the most differentially sensitive sense-organs, and possibly for large alterations in localisation. It is possible that on insensitive parts of the body, and with alterations of position so small as to be near the differential threshold, there would be little to inhibit such reassociation.

We may now consider a few likely criticisms. First, the validity of the mechanical analogy is sure to be questioned.

It will be objected that calculating machines are made by men, who decide exactly what the machine shall be capable of, whereas man is not so made. Those who advance this view seem to think that babies arrive from nowhere, instead of being largely and possibly entirely made by biochemical processes for which the parents deserve at least some credit. They may not know what they are doing, but neither does the operative who 'makes' parts for an aeroplane engine on a semi-automatic lathe. Further, it is not true that a calculating machine gives out no more than its designer put into it; he usually designs it in order that it *shall* do something he cannot—*vide* the Bush differential analyser. Even in a wireless set it is possible, by making a mistake in the wiring, to obtain effects which it may require the best brains to diagnose, if they are required simply to think out the cause of the malfunctioning.

I think it will be agreed by everyone that an explanation is not an explanation at all if it requires as many formulae as there are phenomena; the very essence of explanation is generalisation. The point of divergence between this and opposing views probably lies in looking for things 'in between' cause and effect. The relational type of explanation tends to start with a formula phrased in the language of a particular science and to modify it until it fits a number of facts and seems to express concepts of general application. The mechanist seeks for things in between and may find that these things lead him from the science in which he started into another, as study of combustion led from chemistry (caloric and phlogiston theories) into physics (heat as a form of energy). The mechanist would agree with Butler that 'everything is what it is, and not another thing', but would add that everything is not necessarily what it *seems* at first sight to be. What seems simple may turn out to depend on complicated and apparently dissimilar conditions, as coral reefs depend for their origin and shape on the efforts of Polyzoa; consequently there seems no reason to believe that in seeking for the things in between one may not be led from one science into another. Again, the mechanist does not seek the things in between without reason and gratuitously. He seeks something between two events A and B just because A does not always produce B; and there is no other remedy open to him. This anomaly gives him some of his arguments against the purely relational view and enables him to state why he draws the line at which he ceases to look for more things in between further back than the relationist, and why he is more satisfied with his limit even though it appears to have introduced further complications. If heat merely made a poker red, I do not think any physicist would worry about the intervening stages; he would probably take it as an ultimate fact, and try to advance from that fact to see how much ground he could cover in terms of it. But a little heat makes a poker able to melt wax, more makes it look red, still more yellow. It is this diversity of effects which leads him to enquire into the processes occurring between heat and redness, and to find only two in the end—molecular or atomic vibrations and electromagnetic waves. Any quantities of these, acting on any quantities of matter, always have the same effect, viz. to produce vibrations so that the total energy, though differently distributed, is the same in amount as before. Hypothesis or discovery concerned with things in between arises invariably as a result of the discovery of anomalies as the law of gravitation arises from the anomalies which result from treating planets at different distances from the sun as being acted on by the same force. Nothing is known about the 'mechanism' of a gravitational field itself, largely because few anomalies have been found; if some substance were discovered which 'insulated' bodies from each other's gravitational fields, something would be postulated 'in between' cause and effect, as dielectric constants and conductivities are postulated in electrical theory. Thus it would appear that the scientist is often driven to postulate things in between and should be at liberty to do so until no further anomalies arise. But it is still possible that the method has disadvantages—that for every extra step he interpolates in a process his explanation loses in power to explain the process as a whole. Now there plainly are many methods in statistics, physics, relativity, and so forth, which explain a great deal at a highly relational level. Each of them can deal with phenomena on a scale so large that atomic mechanics would be unable to cope with them. But each is bound to make certain assumptions about the fixity, size, etc., of the atom or individual, which *might* be incorrect. Experiments on the atom give direct data on its nature and largely allay the fear that the higher structure is founded upon sand. If the relation of these higher organisations to the units is understood, there is much less fear of our being faced by a sudden and complete anomaly.

Again, it may be said that I, like the logical positivists, have called many problems unreal—problems of the self, of being, of mind, of objects, of substance and attribute and so forth. But I do not merely retire into a more cautious position; I have tried to produce a verifiable theory as to why these concepts and the problems about them arose, admitting that they are useful up to a point; and I offer an explanation because after all these problems are admitted to be in an unsatisfactory state. Thus I do not simply call them unreal or explain them away. Neither have I just evaded the problems by refusing to express them exactly enough; I have tried to substitute a more exact, because experimentally verifiable, formulation. Finally, with regard to the hylozoistic treatment of consciousness, I can plead that the existence of consciousness as an attribute of organised matter has never been either proved or disproved.

To summarise the whole argument: Explanation, to the man in the street, means giving the causes of things and saying why they happen; and he is sure he perceives these external lasting things, though he may be mistaken about them on particular occasions. I have advanced arguments which seem to support these views. I have not claimed to give a logical proof of the existence of the external world nor of causal action; that, I contend, is continually shown by the fact that experiment is possible at all. But I have tried to show that the causal view is at least more reasonable than any other, that one is entitled to say that the 'given' is already relational, particularly in its spatial aspects. I have suggested that Humean scepticism and the relational explanation of modern physics are both self-contradictory—the first because, though sceptical of all else, it assumes the ability of words to symbolise events, an assumption no better and no worse than that of causation, and the second because the association of definite probabilities with events is founded on the theory of probability, and the fundamental theorems of this are based on the assumption of rigid causality.

But the final proof of anything must come from experience; thus the precision of the old *a priori* philosophies is fallacious in the light of modern criticism and experimental science. The verbal and formal precision of the symbolic logicians and logical positivists seems to be the last trace of this *a priorism* and fated to yield to an experimental approach in which attempts at precise but sterile definition yield to a richer experimental use of words and data as indefinite but fruitful fields for investigation and experiment.

Assuming then the existence of the external world I have outlined a symbolic theory of thought, in which the nervous system is viewed as a calculating machine capable of modelling or paralleling external events, and have suggested that this process of paralleling is the basic feature of thought and of explanation. The possessor of a nervous system is thus able to anticipate events instead of making invariable empirical trial. Such a view is tentatively applied to a number of philosophical and psychological problems (such as paradox and illusion) where ontological explanations, in my opinion, have failed. Here this view affords perhaps some hope of aetiological explanation. Finally, a few possible experimental methods for testing such theories are reviewed and some criticisms considered. I hope, however, that experiment will be thought the final arbiter. And so, *Tentare*.

REFERENCES

Ayer, A. J. 1940. *The Foundations of Empirical Knowledge*. Macmillan and Co., London.

Berkeley, G. *First Dialogue of Hylas and Philonous*. Everyman Edition.

Blanchard, B. 1939. *The Nature of Thought*, vol. 2, p. 381.

Born, M. 1937. *Atomic Physics*, pp. 89–90. Black, London.

Descartes, R. *Discourse on Method*. Everyman Edition.

Edgeworth, F. Y. 1926. Article on 'Probability', Part I, Sec. 1 in *Ency. Brit.* 13th ed. London.

Foley, J. R. 1937. *J. Gen. Psych.* vol. 16, p. 491.

Haldane, J. B. S. 1938. *The Marxist Philosophy and the Sciences*, p. 43. Allen and Unwin, London.

Hawkins, D. J. B. 1937. *Causality and Implication*, p. 50. Sheed and Ward, London.

Helmholtz, H. von. *Physiological Optics*, Eng. trans. vol. 3, p. 532. Opt. Soc. Amer.

Hume, D. *A Treatise of Human Nature*. Everyman Edition.

Kemp-Smith, N. *Commentary to Kant's Critique of Pure Reason*.

Laplace, P. S. *Théorie analytique des probabilités*, Liv. 2, Ch. 1, No. 1.

Lashley, K. S. 1938. *J. Gen. Psychol.* vol. 18, p. 123.

Lashley, K. S. 1941. *Biological Symposia*, vol. 7, pp. 302. Jaques Cattell Press.

Love, A. E. H. 1926. *Ency. Brit.* vol. 14, p. 535.

MacCurdy, J. T. 1928. *Common Principles in Physiology and Psychology*.

Northrop, F. S. C. 1931. *Science and First Principles*, p. 284. Cambridge.

Pascal, B. *Pensées*. Everyman Edition.

Plato, *Republic*, Bk. 1.

Pledge, H. T. 1939. *Science since 1500*. H.M. Stationery Office.

Stebbing, L. S. 1937. *Philosophy and the Physicists*, p. 183. Methuen, London.

Stevens, S. S. 1935. *Amer. J. Psychol.* vol. 47, p. 323.

Whitehead, A. N. 1925. *The Principles of Natural Knowledge*.

Whitehead, A. N. and Russell, B. A. W. 1910. *Principia Mathematica*.

(Not specifically mentioned in text)

Campbell, N. R. 1928. *Measurement and Calculation*. Longmans, London.

Eddington, A. 1928. *The Nature of the Physical World*.

Ewing, A. C. 1932–3. *Arist. Soc. Proc.* vol. 33, p. 95.

Geldard, F. A. 1939. *Psychol. Rev.* vol. 46, p. 411.
Hull, C. L. 1937. *Psychol. Rev.* vol. 44, p. 1.
Jeans, J. 1930. *The Mysterious Universe.*
Jeffreys, H. 1937. *Scientific Inference.* Cambridge.
Johnson, H. M. 1939. *Psychol. Rev.* vol. 46, p. 492.
Keynes, J. M. 1921. *A Treatise on Probability.*
Ogden, C. K. and Richards, I. A. 1923. *The Meaning of Meaning.*
Pearson, K. *The Grammar of Science.* Everyman Edition.
Stout, G. F. 1935. *Arist. Soc. Suppl. Proc.* pp. 51–3.
Westaway, F. W. *Scientific Method.* Blackie, London.
Wisdom, J. 1938. *Mind,* pp. 468–81.
Woodger, J. H. 1929. *Biological Principles.*